Also by

Christie Y. Shaw

- Becoming The Person You Told People You Were
- The Boy and The Man He Became
- Good Relationships, Bad Relationships: What is the Common Denominator?

Be Who You Say You Are

THE SEQUEL TO BECOMING THE PERSON YOU TOLD PEOPLE YOU WERE

Foreword by Omar D. Shaw

CHRISTIE Y. SHAW

Copyright © 2023 Christie Y. Shaw.

All rights reserved. No part of this book may be used or reproduced by any means, graphic, electronic, or mechanical, including photocopying, recording, taping or by any information storage retrieval system without the written permission of the author except in the case of brief quotations embodied in critical articles and reviews.

This book is a work of non-fiction. Unless otherwise noted, the author and the publisher make no explicit guarantees as to the accuracy of the information contained in this book and in some cases, names of people and places have been altered to protect their privacy.

Archway Publishing books may be ordered through booksellers or by contacting:

Archway Publishing
1663 Liberty Drive
Bloomington, IN 47403
www.archwaypublishing.com
844-669-3957

Because of the dynamic nature of the Internet, any web addresses or links contained in this book may have changed since publication and may no longer be valid. The views expressed in this work are solely those of the author and do not necessarily reflect the views of the publisher, and the publisher hereby disclaims any responsibility for them.

Any people depicted in stock imagery provided by Getty Images are models, and such images are being used for illustrative purposes only.
Certain stock imagery © Getty Images.

Scripture quotations marked CSB have been taken from the Christian Standard Bible®, Copyright © 2017 by Holman Bible Publishers. Used by permission. Christian Standard Bible® and CSB® are federally registered trademarks of Holman Bible Publishers.

Scripture quotations marked ESV are from the ESV Bible® (The Holy Bible, English Standard Version®), copyright © 2001 by Crossway Bibles, a publishing ministry of Good News Publishers. Used by permission. All rights reserved.

Scripture quotations marked KJV are taken from the Holy Bible, King James Version.

Scripture quotations marked NIV are taken from the Holy Bible, New International Version®, NIV®. Copyright © 1973, 1978, 1984 by Biblica, Inc.™ Used by permission of Zondervan. All rights reserved worldwide.

ISBN: 978-1-6657-4126-2 (sc)
ISBN: 978-1-6657-4143-9 (e)

Library of Congress Control Number: 2023905584

Print information available on the last page.

Archway Publishing rev. date: 05/03/2023

For My Baby Brother
Michael L. Shaw
#9

In Loving Memory of My Mother
Dorthy Rosetta Shaw

Contents

Foreword ix
Preface: *Poetic Perspective* xi
Introduction: *If I Can Help Somebody* xiii

Chapter 1:　Emotionally Edited 1
  - *Girl Interrupted*
  - *My Mother*
  - *Became What I Yearned For*
  - *2022 West 4th Street*
  - *Leaving Home*
  - *Love-Relationships, Marriage & Singleness*
  - *About My Baby Brother*
  - *Michael Worshiped Him*

Chapter 2:　We Are Here Now 53

Chapter 3:　Homeless 56

Chapter 4:　Higher Version of Self 61

Chapter 5:　Un-Stuck 65

Chapter 6:　Do What You Say You Do 69

Chapter 7:　Gifts, Talents & Things 73
  - *Highly Visible*

Chapter 8:   A Journey 80
- *Trajectory*
- *Renaissance*
- *Purpose*

Chapter 9:   One Commandment Corp 93
- *Matters of the Heart*

Chapter 10: A Half Dozen or So or Nine
             Months to Grow 104

Resources 117
About the Author 119
References 121

Foreword

When I was asked to write this foreword, I was confronted with quite a few thoughts. "What do I say," "Am I even capable of doing this," and "Why me?" to name a few. After struggling to come up with effective words, I decided that looking up exactly what a foreword should cover might be beneficial. This bright idea was a tremendous help from a technical standpoint, but even more so in answering the aforementioned questions. As the son of the author, realizing my capabilities and "answering the bell" when called are values that I have learned from my mother.

In a stream of consciousness that began with pondering the current and future successes of myself and my siblings and how to build something that spans generations, I found myself fixated on some early childhood memories. Traumatic memories of experiences I endured alongside my mother. "What must it be like for a woman in those situations," I wondered. Not just any woman, but my mother. Thinking about her losing her own mother at an unfathomable age, giving birth while still a child herself, and navigating landmines disguised as men. This all prompted me to text "Mom, you are quite the success story. People don't beat the odds the way you did."

Often in film there is a complementary character to help guide the protagonist to realizing their ultimate potential. It makes for great storytelling; especially when the protagonist faces what seems to be insurmountable odds. While there may have been people to help push her along; through a (sometimes stubborn) sense of pride, ambition, and desire to be her best self my mother has managed to be that character for herself while never losing sight of the fact that reaching her ultimate potential demands that she shares her journey in a way that benefits others.

Omar D. Shaw

Preface
POETIC PERSPECTIVE

Not sure if to feel if it's a conclusion or an illusion or perhaps a combination of both... besides "life is but a dream" so if that's the case, perhaps that's the illusion and reality is like a Spike Lee Joint yelling, "wake up" and maybe then, I can rest my mind a bit and climb out of this restless pit... cause this dream of a life got me racing and running behind time waving a script—in the air that reads, "would of, could of, should of" ... yelling, while jumping over hurdles "Hold up, wait for me, I'm trying to get some things done, so I can take care of my family!" Besides, 'life is but a dream" should end the way I dream it to, but that ain't the way it's going—time keeps right on running like it don't hear me ... don't even slow down so I can catch up... a head start would have been nice since time was running before I got here, but no its gone on about its business and doing what it do... keeping me chasing for a clue. Now this darn boy done blindsided me and switched up the birth order—got it looking like I am the last in line when in "reality" #8 is followed by #9 – ain't no such thing as 8 minus 9 *that's a negative balance*, so I'm feeling emptied out… drained by thoughts of this tragic conclusion or a bad illusion that #9 was here and now he's not, and now something feels exposed… the insulation is gone—and no longer separated by 800 – 900 miles, or even radio silence—but by an eternity. And I don't know if that's a conclusion or an illusion, but I tell you what I feel—feels like time, is that sand slipping through my hand bit by bit… so that tells me that I'm not running behind time—I'm running out of it.

Introduction
IF I CAN HELP SOMEBODY

Writing this book has taken on several formats, ideas, suggestions, but none of them stuck until now—until I went back to following my style and instinct for writing. Until I did that, a process that I have never found to be cumbersome or difficult seemingly became just that. It had become difficult for me until the morning, (no coincidence following prayer the night before), I had an epiphany to rid myself of "other people's" ideas, scrap the initial, nearly completed manuscript, and begin again. Immediately the writing airwaves opened up in the way that I am accustomed—the flow and instinctive writing style that I have enjoyed—the writing ability that I know is "my gift." So, I want to start with this suggestion for anyone that reads this book—remain true to your gifting. Treat your gift, and talent as if you are in a relationship because you are. So, cultivate it, develop it, and remain loyal to it. This does not mean you are not to refine, and enhance your God-given talents and gifting, but you never want to lose connection with your core, authentic style that makes what you do you. It's easy in a world compartmentalized into "influencers" and "followers" to forget that you are uniquely equipped to be who you are, and to offer what you have to offer.

Shortly after I released my last book, "Becoming The Person You Told People You Were", I was a guest on a radio show to do an Author's Roundtable session, and the host asked everyone about their challenges with "writer's block", and at my turn, I confidently responded, "I don't have that challenge. I haven't experienced it, because my writing comes fluidly, and easily to me." And then it happened—as if to rebut my confident assertion, I got hit by the "block." However, what I realize now is while I was working on this book, I thought it was a good idea to "follow", and join a social media writing community platform, so I did. I would later realize that I was taking in, consuming the ideas, and concepts of other writers that in no way complimented or shared my "innate" writing approach. These writers, though talented, did not look at writing through the lens of a "God-given" gifting, talent, or instinct, but rather an acquired skill—something they were taught. Additionally, they viewed writing as a career choice vs it being their "purpose." So, this experience brought me back to the revelation that at the core of my writing is the mission to reach, help, enhance, the emotional well-being of someone else—even if it's one person.

For as long as I can remember, "If I can help somebody with a word or song, if I can help somebody as I pass along, then my living shall not be in vain", from the song written by, Alma Androzzo and made famous through the vocals of the late Mahalia Jackson, has been a song, mantra, and guiding principle that has guided my interactions and writing. So, it's from this premise that I will always write. Consequently, choosing to write from this place of instinct, and purpose instead of learnt skill will always require resilience, courage, and transparency if it is to have an impact of encouragement and inspiration for those that read my work.

The initial plan was that this book would be the official sequel to "Becoming The Person You Told People You Were"—it was also that thought process that seemingly got in the way of creative flow. Because I wanted to deliver on my ideas of writing a sequel the process became one of overthinking and was stifling my ability to "just write" because I was focused on writing content that would finish telling or add more substance to what was written previously—which I also felt obligated to do because of feedback that I received from readers of my last book. They wanted to know more.

But the morning I awakened with the thought to just write as if my previous book had never been written, I felt liberated and released to do what did not feel forced and scripted. And I think as the reader, you may appreciate this uninhibited journey that will unfold over the course of the next few pages.

Admittedly, "Becoming The Person You Told People You Were", is succinct in its style, yet it's substantial, and it has seemingly encouraged many readers based on feedback and reviews which means my intent was accomplished. But I admit—more detail could have been shared, detail that would allow for readers to see more of themselves in my humanness, especially women. What I wrote in my last book were the stories of "how I have overcome", and "this is where I am now." But it's a sure thing that life is a continuous journey as long as we are living it, and by no means is it a final destination until we've finished it. So, the journey is not without the stuff in-between, and sometimes, for many of us, it's a bit yucky, messy, complicated, and in some instances embarrassing. But by no means does any of the ebbs and flows of a journey disqualify us from showing up as and becoming better or the best versions of ourselves, despite the fact that people will treat you otherwise—because people have a human tendency to want to hold you in place to the lower seasons or versions of yourself. So perhaps it's better stated here, what I thought to include in a different chapter, that if you find yourself making statements like, "That seems like a lofty goal or considering that you are, or I remember when you, he or she used to or when I met you, you did not have, do or wasn't…", be mindful of that coming from you and coming at you—this is a clear indication of what I like to refer to as framing someone hostage to a time in their lives that may not have been the best display of who and what they could potentially be or do with their lives—but that never negates a better future version of who and what anyone can do or be.

Many years ago, I sat with my, late, uncle discussing an indictment that someone made about me following some explosive details, I shared in my very first book—her response was a combination of vitriol and judgement because of what I exposed about a family member's attempt to violate me as a child, an experience I had as a very young girl in a relationship that I had no business being in. What she said, could have altered the way I felt and thought of myself and possibly how I would view my future—until my uncle said this one thing in my defense that changed my entire perspective, "*I spoke to her about that, and I asked her to think of the most embarrassing, shameful thing she's ever done even that thing people don't know about— and after you do that, then tell me if you would want to be judged for the rest of your life based on that*?" Think about that... I think that's what it is to have a judgement about someone with a beam in your own eye. We are all faulty people—and we are all prone to applying limitations or judgements onto others because of how we have limited and see ourselves.

In "*Becoming The Person You Told People You Were*", there is a chapter titled "*Critically Necessary*", pg. 57), where I speak about the necessity of "criticism" which isn't with the same connotation as what the young people refer to as "hating on." So, it's worth reiterating that counsel and critique is "*critically necessary*", but criticism laced with jealousy, resentment and devaluing language is not critique—it's malice.

So, I stress—know the difference between the two because quality of counsel when giving it and receiving can change the course of someone's life rightly or wrongly.

Chapter 1
EMOTIONALLY EDITED

"Good stories deal with our moral struggles, our uncertainties, our dreams, or blunders, our contradictions, our endless quest for understanding."

—Tim O'Brien, Novelist

So, I started the initial draft of this book bent on a specific narrative that would not revisit past traumatic experiences because my intent is to speak from a "better" place and because my goal through writing is to help inspire, motivate, and encourage growth and forward movement with my readers. But after a recent discussion with my daughter, I had to ask myself, "forward movement from what?"

"Mom you could have a bestseller if you shared with readers what you've been through, really be transparent—down to earth. Let people know what you have been

through so they know that you can relate, and they are not the first and only to have their experience." What is interesting about Jasmine's advice is that I thought I did that. I thought that's what I did in my writing, but the truth is "Becoming The Person You Told People You Were", was emotionally edited. I wrote from a point of arrival without sharing why the point of arrival was worth writing about in the first place. I shared only in-part, in a compartmentalized way. I was pulled into deep thought after that discussion with my daughter because what she was referring to without really saying it was—"write about the trauma, write about the heartbreak, love, loss, desires, even loneliness."

Because I was doing what we do as African Americans, especially what African American women have a tendency to do—sharing experiences of godliness, steadfastness, overcoming, resilience, and arrival, but doing so without the details of how and why. So, prior to getting to the "where I am now" phase of this "sequel" (that may not read like much of a sequel). I want to share some details around where I have been and what I have been through, with the hope of providing clarity around why I share—why I write. Consequently, you may feel that you are reading two different books from two different people and maybe that's because you are.

Will Smith's bestselling autobiography still hail as one of the best autobiographies that I have ever read—it was then followed by the "Slap." The slap literally heard around the world from the grand stage of the 2022 Oscar Award Celebration. And like so many, I am confident that

I experienced an array of emotion that ranged from shock, disappointment, and even anger.

But here-in lies not just Will Smith's truth, but "our" truths—the trauma that African Americans have had to "get over, "forget about" "keep moving beyond", even turn into energy towards overachievement—and perceived perfection—does not go away on its own, if at all. And that's what we as a race of people have been trying to do for hundreds of years—in some instances it morphs into drug usage, alcohol and repeated, abusive learned behaviors. We were taught to wear a mask, love, respect, and forgive our molesters who are oftentimes family members—and put makeup over our black eyes from the domestic abuse and keep moving. Violent death and murder of our children and loved ones is trauma that we have been braced to normalize. And in the case of Will Smith who prior to his phenomenally-written, bestselling book, disclosed the trauma and devastating effects of the domestic violence imposed on his mother by his father. On the heels of that book's success, he was receiving a well-deserved, long-awaited award that represented the pinnacle of an actor's success. But in the forefront of everyone's knowledge now—is knowing how Will shared that he felt like a self-proclaimed "coward" for not defending and protecting his mother-according to him, something he never got over. So, a joke told at the expense of his wife by the incomparable comedian, actor, and Oscar Host, Chris Rock, suddenly became the catalyst for Will's need to redeem himself. But this display of assault was one of the many ways that unresolved trauma shows up—no matter how many years later. And in Will's case it was freshly unearthed because of the recent writing and release of his autobiography. Will's internal conflict displayed the night of the Oscars was a visual of Romans 7:15 ESV

"...For I do not understand my own actions. For I do not do what I want, but I do the very thing I hate."

This is a spiritual law the bible teaches, and while I am sure we can all point to our own personal and individual internal conflicts—the night of the 2022 Oscars was a vivid depiction of what that looks and feels like.

Before I finished this book, Chris Rock broke his silence because up until this point he had not said much—at least not publicly. But according to an article written in the Huffington Post, (Mazza, E., September 6, 2022), Rock expressed his thoughts about the video that Smith released offering an apology, citing that during a "gig at London's Q2 Arena, according to Deadline", the comedian said, "F*$#k your hostage video." Apparently, Rock also stated, "Smith impersonated "a perfect man' for 30 years before revealing that he was 'just as ugly as the rest of us" (The Guardian, Shoard, C, Sept. 5, 2022). And it's this statement that resonates with me because isn't that just like us who are taught to mask, pretend, deny, and even strive for excellence, as if achieving excellence is some type of perfumed antidote to cover our stinky, messy, trauma. And the "just as ugly" is code for just as broken, just as traumatized, and just like many of us vacillating and managing being 'in and out of our 'right' minds' because of previous trauma— [phrase borrowed from a book by the same title] (Columbia University Press, Editors; Brown, D., & Keith, V., 2003).

GIRL INTERRUPTED

So, my trauma… but before we go there, I want to share that in the recent past, someone said to me, *"You've shared the stories of your past enough, everyone knows your story. It's time to move on."* I realize now that is another reason why I wrote *"Becoming The Person You Told People You Were"* with such a *"I am here now"* approach. I started the initial draft of this book doing it again—of removing that narrative despite knowing it would provide more perspective and context for my reader. But again, people's advice, and opinions are given through the lens of their own perspectives, experiences, and however they chose to live with or through those experiences. But it's precisely that—it's theirs. So I will share and reshare for however long it's relevant, for as many generations I am afforded to do so because I learned something recently, and that is younger women are gleaning from my writings too, it's not just the people that have known me from times past—my readers are not limited to my social circle, otherwise there would be no need to write books when I could just share via text messages or phone calls.

I read a social media post recently that quoted Author of "Parent Hacks", Asha Dornfest, *"I think new writers are too worried that it has all been said before. Sure, it has, but not by you."* And my response to that is, sure it has, but we all have a different sphere of influence. There is place in time that's divinely and specifically assigned to each person in the earth to offer their individual gifts no matter if it's acting, singing, reading, writing, or tennis—all for a collective purpose. Imagine if Dr. Angelou did not write because James Baldwin shared the same sentiments, or LaVar Burton didn't create a culture and platform of reading books because Mr. Rodgers had the same concept, or Venus or Serena Williams didn't play tennis because Author Ashe played with the same mastery and techniques. There are generations who have no idea of the other while the latter impacted their lives.

MY MOTHER

> SHAW, DOROTHY R.
> On January 7, 1972. Of 502 W. 4th St. Wife of Jesse, Sr., mother of Ronald, Jesse, Jr., Dennis, David, Michael, Debra, Christie, Marianne Townsend, & Valerie Richardson. Daughter of Elsie Wilson. Sister of William, Robert, LeFenus, Rodney, Donald & Alvin Wilson, Ann Corbitt, Ruth Wilson and Elizabeth Richardson.
> Relatives and friends are invited to attend the funeral service Wednesday, 2 o'clock from Faith Tabernacle Church, 3rd & Fulton St. Friends may call the same day at the Church from 11 a.m. to 2 p.m. Interment Greenlawn Cemetery.

So that said, on the mornings of February 7th, every single year, I don't need any reminders of my momma's birthdate because it's a date that's engrained on my soul—obviously not because it was a date I got to celebrate with her as my older siblings may have, but because it's the date that marks the date of her birth, and therefore a date that became as special to me as any other memorable date on the calendar. I was only seven when my mom tragically passed on January 7th, 1972—a date that now feels even more cruel because she was found dead on the morning of her baby boy's (my baby brother's) Michael's 5th birthday. He too is now gone from amongst us—with a tragic end.

This is not the first time I have visited this story about the death of my mother. The first time I did so was in 1996 - 97 by way of a book I wrote titled, *"Good Relationships, Bad Relationships… What's the Common Denominator?"* As a result, I raised the ire of siblings and other family members, and seemingly lost their "affections." But my resolve today as it relates specifically to those few siblings; I never had their respect or affections to lose—because the generation gaps between me and my older siblings and our not being raised together during those critical years, with the others—due to our separation after our mom's death created a different kind of gap that would require that we got to know each other on our own terms—which if I am to be totally honest—never worked out regardless of the parental blood ties we shared. Just like how not every person you meet will become your friend—the same applied, and the older I got the clearer that became for me. However, I will add that the offense that I caused my oldest living brother and my now deceased youngest brother Michael, is something I am sorry about. Nevertheless, I don't regret what I wrote—especially when I believed greater costs were at stake—and healing was that greater cost—not just for me, but for my children. Families keep secrets—they hide truths that are the solutions to someone else's well-being—the answers to critical questions that need to be answered, generational bondage, outcomes, and learned behaviors that leave subset of families grappling with issues that they believe lie totally with them because of their mere existence and that's not true, it's not fair, and it's not good.

So, I don't know for sure, but I imagine that the meeting of my mother and father entailed a great deal of physical attraction. As described by a few different people, they were both beautiful, charismatic, and young. The decision and behaviors of these two young people likely resulted in the flourishing, and evolvement of a relationship that went from chemistry attraction to a fatal one, and abusive in-between. And I am confident that long before my father was on the scene, my mother had already had other traumatic experiences from which I am equally confident she never healed from.

From every account I have heard from older family, friends, associates, uncles, aunts, and a sibling or two; my mother was quite the fighter, and my father was not exempt from her willingness to do so. Nevertheless, I am not sure how that translated into who was the aggressor or not in the numerous domestic fights they exchanged, but I am confident that when he or she was under the influence of alcohol, the violence was perpetuated. My father was not settled in his role as a husband—that is not missed on me. But he drank—she drank, and the outcome was never peaceful. So, while the two beautiful individuals were who they were individually, they were also who they were together, resulting in the bleak conditions passed on to their children, and to the detriment of what could have otherwise been a cohesive family legacy.

The evening of my mother's death, I slept in her bed. I recalled and still recall what I refer to as, "*The Shadow.*" The shadow wore a big-brimmed hat, and it kept trying to enter my mother's room but reverted back because I kept sounding the alarm to my mother that, "*Someone was in the room.*" I asked my mother to bring her feet to the top of the bed because they hung slightly off the bed, and she agreed to do so if I turned my head towards the wall. So, we both did as we agreed. As I slept, my mother must have carried me into my own bed—in the room I shared with my older sister, because I would awaken there the following morning. However, the awakening was to the reality that my mother was dead. The later reality that would be realized was that she did not "*just die.*" And my assertion that I am committed to is that if she had a "*heart attack*", it's because of the physical trauma that was inflicted on her.

The morning of discovery of my mother's death, my brother who is six years my senior and I bickered at the breakfast table—someone went to tell. I'm not sure if it was my brother or my sister, but according to my sister, upon the discovery of my mother's dead body, she ran out of the house in her nightgown to our oldest brother Ronald's home which was very nearby. They simultaneously contacted the other older siblings, all of whom went to my father's job at Baldt & Anchor and according to her, "They frantically requested to speak to him." According to my sister, "When my father arrived at the gate, they told him that "our mother was dead." He responded, according to my sister, "*I know.*" So here is an important account about my father that I learned in following years, he was brutally honest. So, much so that he did not deny knowing his wife—our mother—was dead. Nor did he deny that he was the reason that she was dead.

Years following the death of my mother there was an incident to take place while I was visiting my brother and sister-in-law on the eve before Easter. There were several family members there which is why my aunt allowed me to visit, because it was an opportunity for me to be with my siblings. However, while I sat alone in the living room on the edge of their black and white zebra print sofa, my father, who was intoxicated stumbled into the hallway closet—assuming heading to the bathroom. He whispered my name a couple times until I answered him. When I acknowledged him, he responded, "*I know you know I killed your mother.*" I jumped up and ran all the way home. I told my aunt what happened, and she said, "*I knew it, I knew he killed my sister!*" I have no idea what happened after that.

But nothing changed the fact that I loved our father. Recalling the day, my father and I got into a very heated argument in his home where I was staying temporarily because, by this time, I had long burned the bridge that my aunt was building for me to cross over. During this argument, my father said, "*I know you hate me because you think I killed your mother.*" I responded, "*I know you killed her, but I don't hate you – I love you.*" And he responded, "*I love you too.*" I remember, my now deceased sister, Valerie, asking me, "*How can you say you love him knowing what he did to Dot?*" I responded, "*How could I not love him, he's my father? Besides, she loved him, why can't I?"* And she said nothing after that.

However, I want to elaborate on something here before I move on... what I believe my sister was asking wasn't about loving our dad—it was really a question about forgiveness—and I believe to withhold forgiveness in my case would have been more a matter of picking a side. For my sister it was a result of a lived experience. I didn't live the experience of witnessing and seeing the tumult between our mom and dad—she did. Another thing that I am glad I get to touch on as result of having read a phenomenal book by Timothy Keller, *"Forgive Why Should I and How Can I?"*, before final publishing of this book—is that I understand that the topic of forgiveness is multi-faceted and complex especially in our cancel-culture, zero tolerance society. And forgiveness has always come very naturally for me—so much so, that I too have questioned how and why it has been so easy for me to forgive people even of offenses that would likely be categorized as "unforgiveable." Perhaps I just have not reached my threshold yet, but it appears to be an innate characteristic for me because even before becoming more versed in the concepts and practices of forgiveness via the lens of Christianity I was living it out. However, forgiveness is not the same as passivity. To forgive does not mean remain—it does not remove the pursuit of justice—nor does it render you feeble. I have found forgiveness to be one of the most liberating acts I have ever participated in.

As a very young child my mother escorted and loaded me onto the white church bus weekly, which I have also referred to as a church van. The female pastor who I believe, if my memory serves me correctly, was "*Mother Wortherly.*" She'd drive and park the white church bus at the end of our block where the neighborhood children who could attend did attend and we all listened to the short stories about God of the Bible and ended our attendance with the singing of songs. I would be on that van singing, "*This Little Light of Mine*", and "*Jesus Loves the Little Children*" with all my heart—at the top of my lungs. I do believe it was there on that van where the Spirit of God pierced my heart. Realizing that my mother died when I was seven would mean I was between 5-7 years of age during that time. There are few details that I can recall about my brief time with my mother, but those memories that I do recall are etched in my mind—like how we made ice cream from scratch once outside on the front steps of the housing projects where we lived with an old-fashioned ice cream maker—it had a manual hand crank that she let me turn to mix the ingredients. I also remember that she always held my hand as she walked me to the church bus, or walked me to Franklin Elementary school, or to the doctor where I'd receive my vaccinations for school–wherever we were off to—she never failed to take me by my hand. I also remember her asking me "*Who do you want to live with when I die?*" We sat in the kitchen—with me on her lap on what may have been a wall radiator beneath the kitchen window. I remember the question, but not the voice—its tone, pitch, or sound. I do remember the tick-tock sound of the yellow studded, cat-clock that hung on the wall—its protruding eyes and tail that moved from left to right. But she asked the question and I responded, *"Aunt Ruth."*

And so, the story goes, that many already know, but many do not, which is why it gets repeated here, with my Aunt Ruth, I went to live.

The day that my aunt came to retrieve me followed a night spent at the home of a family friend deemed my "Godmother." Miss Johnnie Mae was her name. Similar, to my mother, she was a tall, fair-skinned, beautiful woman. I spent the night in her home with her and her children. One of which was named Dina. Dina was a mild-mannered, pretty-faced girl with a generous deep-dimpled smile. It seemed that she smiled a lot, and she should have because it was one of her most beautiful traits—it was a beautiful smile that put a seven-year-old child at ease about spending the night in a strange home—a child clueless about the concept of death, and even more clueless about the reality that she would never be returning home, nor would she see her mother again—at least not alive.

To further comfort me Dina promised to take me for donuts in the morning, to what is still a renowned bakery in the city of Chester Pennsylvania— "Ann's Donuts" since renamed and owned by a different owner for many years now, "Phatso's", fifty years later is still going strong —some of the best tasting donuts in the local region. Excited as any child could be with anticipation, I could hardly sleep for thinking about going for donuts in the morning. Morning finally arrived and off we were, and as we strolled off my aunt would arrive to retrieve me. Dina was completely deflated as my aunt explained that I had to leave with her. I remember her sadden facial expression clearly—her generous smile disappeared, and her eyes widen as she pled for enough time to take me to "Ann's", but my aunt denied her request.

So, while I did not know what or how to describe my feelings then, I have the understanding now to know that I was crushed and deeply sadden from that experience. And at the risk of sounding melodramatic, I processed and carried that experience well into my adulthood. It would show up in my later behaviors as haste—when hurrying our rushing to do certain things because, I feared something would interrupt me before I could get them done. I processed feelings of anxiety that as soon as I get to the day or a date that something significant or good was supposed to take place—it wouldn't. It took years to unravel that. It appeared that soon after my arrival at my aunt's home, I would attend my mother's funeral which at that time, I am confident I comprehended this too meant she wasn't *coming to get me*, and that I now *lived* with Aunt Ruth. That day it rained as we stood in the cemetery at the burial. I remember the rain. I remember my outfit, a white (maybe cream) dress and matching topcoat trimmed in green, extremely tight curls in my short hair, and I remember hearing a "voice" in my ears—my mind—my spirit as I stood there… "*I will take care of you.*" Too young to understand and certainly I had no reason or no one to tell it to. It wasn't until many years later, between fourteen and fifteen years old, my aunt released me from her care at 2022 West 4th street. It would appear, I wore out my welcome as I struggled through identity, familial, and emotional conflicts. Nevertheless, as I walked towards wherever I was lying my head during that time, looking down at the ground, pushing the grass with my foot as if kicking a ball, and I heard that "voice" again, *"I will take care of you."* So, much of my life during that time was turbulent. I went from pillar to post as the idiom goes, but no real "home" per se. Other than at my aunt's for approximately seven years, the longest tenure or anything that felt like "home" was with my father, which was also short-lived, but long enough to provide enough stability to get through and graduate high school, having become a teenage mother. Eventually, though very young, I would get my own apartment in a newly built subsidized apartment complex called Chester Apartments. I knew nothing about being fiscally responsible for managing a household. You might say, I was growing up on the fly and doing so was tumultuous to say the least, but at this point in my life, there is no attempt at blame towards anyone—but I have come to understand that conditions are indeed passed on—good or bad.

But here's what I know for sure, trauma leaves wounds and consequences—pretending that it doesn't just perpetuates it. I spent many years trying to behave as if "nothing was wrong with me" because the very sound of that statement— *"nothing wrong with me"*, made me feel inadequate, and that's the lie that's been passed on for far too long for so many generations throughout the African American community.

Now imagine—watching a movie fifty years following the death of your mother and bursting into tears, and not understanding why. But at this point in my life, I have the depth of understanding to know why. But so often in our culture many of us are never afforded an opportunity to learn of the effects that buried trauma has.

The movie was titled, "*God's Compass*" (2016), not necessarily a spectacular movie, but it was one of those good for the soul—feel good type of movies that I enjoy watching. The storyline was of a widow (spiritual, God-fearing) woman, Mrs. Suzanne Waters, who felt that there was a deep calling for her to take in a young man who, interestingly, was attempting to steal her daughter's car, that was pulled over, something he did only to take care of himself and his baby sister following the death of his mother and father who died in a car crash—leaving them orphaned and homeless. When Eli discovers the daughter still in the car in premature labor, an unintended consequence was he was thief turned hero for getting her to the hospital—saving both her and the baby. But recognized by the police for being wanted for prior car thefts, he was arrested, therefore not making it back to the abandoned building that he and his baby sister stayed in. Mrs. Waters attended his court hearing and volunteered to take him in, not realizing that he came with a little sister. Before all of this happened, he told his little sister to, "*go home*" when she wandered out of the abandoned building that they were squatting in to follow him while he looked for a car to steal. After being released into Mrs. Waters' care, Eli stole her car, but it was to try to find his baby sister Naomi. After days of feverishly searching all the community with no success, he'd return to Mrs. Waters' home telling her for the first time that he had a baby sister, and she was gone. The entire church community got involved in a multi-city search until Eli and another character came upon the home that was once Eli and Naomi's old home. Greeted at the door by an eccentric female homeowner that did welcome Naomi in, and was expecting Eli because Naomi told her, "*He will come get me*". Upon seeing his adorable little sister, he asked, "*What made you come here?*" Naomi sheepishly replied, revealing her one missing tooth, "*You said, go home.*"

I erupted into tears! I said out loud, "Why in the world am I crying like this?" And immediately, I connected my emotions to, "*You said go home.*" That moment unearthed the reality that for fifty years, I can still feel emotion about my mother not coming home—after fifty years I still carry the effects of her not "*coming to get me.*"

BECAME WHAT I YEARNED FOR

So much of adulthood is managing or compartmentalizing the influences of our childhoods—good or bad. Parenting my own children took years of figuring out, faltering, failings, and continuous progress towards something that would eventually look and feel right—not perfect, but right. I can see the differences of the various stages of my (evolving) parenting abilities—in some phases the lack thereof—in each of their individual outcomes.

I dedicated my last book to my children noting that "*I have had the honor of parenting them, and the privilege of learning from them*" (Shaw, 2021), and nothing could be truer. It's been an honor because their lives have been paramount to defining and refining mine, especially my oldest son. And the reason I say, "especially" him is because I was a child when I had him, and I had no idea of the magnitude of responsibility and care that he not only needed but deserved—as all children do. One of the many conditions that resulted from my interrupted childhood and start in life, was this overwhelming need to have and love someone that would love me back. I was fourteen when I entered my first relationship with a man that was six years my senior—a relationship that followed being released from the home at 2022 West 4th street. Prior to meeting him, I also had a best friend that was in a relationship with someone six years her senior, and by no means am I deflecting, but that somehow normalized the inappropriate age mismatch in my mind. I would later learn she was being physically abused when I saw her blackened eye through her makeup, which would turn out to be one of many to follow.

During that time shelter for me was very erratic and so was I. For a few years I was involved in that awful relationship, now those details I will not repeat, but know it was an awful relationship. The fact that I did not succumb to his attempts to completely defile me is nothing short of God's grace—nothing short of a miracle. Once I decided to get out of that relationship, I entered another, which I knew was an unhealthy transition from one relationship to another, though not dangerous like the previous. In this relationship my son was conceived, and I was strategically okay with that. "*Baby syndrome*" was something that I referred to as the need to gratify and fill a void for unconditional love, and though the love for my child was unmatched—a void did still exist, because I was trying to fill the void of needing and missing my own mother. The larger reality was that this child's life would require more of me than I could have ever thought because I was in no way emotionally equipped, mature enough, nor did I have adequate financial means therefore making life harder than it needed to be for both of us. And I don't want to minimize the gravity of the impact of being a teenage, unwed mother in the event a young girl is reading this because it's not to be minimized in any way. But I was very aware that I needed God—not at all in a cliché kind of way, but as an absolute truth. I could not raise this child outside of an intentional relationship with God. It became clear to me quickly that I had to be guided, governed, even protected, and doing so would require a deliberate effort on my part. And with the sincerest of intentions, I accepted Christ. But it would be a progression over the course of many years before I grew from a "Christian" into a student of His Word, precepts, and principles.

So, in between time there were other relationships—one of which was another awful one, which was seemingly becoming a pathology—a marriage that from its inception was abusive, suffocating, and short-lived. I got out quickly because one thing I was sure of was that I was not going to repeat my mother's outcomes, nor would I subject my now two children to witnessing ongoing domestic violence. I am privileged to have children that are wonderful human beings, and though not without internal struggles and normal life-related challenges, they are smart, educated formally and organically, compassionate, generous, entrepreneurial, industrious, people who defy the outcomes that "could have been", considering that I was growing up myself while parenting them.

However, the pathology of unhealthy relationships for me had really become a thing, until something shifted within me. And I can't state the date or year, but I remember the feeling—the shift, but it would not be before my third (youngest) child would be conceived. I remember a cold morning knelt beside my bed fully dressed for work in a pink wool pleated Jones of New York skirt and a navy-blue blouse—praying and asking God to deliver me from whatever it was that kept me in this pattern of unhealthy, unfulfilling, and devaluing relationships. I spent five years in a different relationship that would follow that prayer, and though it was by far the most stable—eventually it was clear that it was not God's best for me. So, I released him—we released each other. And today, what I hope for and wait for as God's best for me still has not been realized—*or maybe it has.*

2022 WEST 4ᵀᴴ STREET

Recently, I listened to various stories by adults who are just now telling their stories of childhood molestation. Some of them still wearing the scars, further exasperated by alcohol, drugs, and sex, and others living productive, substantial lives, but are still only a story away from its truth—meaning it may be in the past, but it's never forgotten.

Kendrick Lamar, who I hail as one of the most prolific, brilliant, and gifted lyricist-rappers of his time, released a cut on his latest CD titled, Mr. Morale & The Big Steppers (2022), titled, "United in Grief." It starts with, *"I hope you find some peace of mind in this lifetime,"* and carries its listener along on a journey of how grief and depression is camouflaged with large grandiose purchases, Sex and other behaviors that exhibit mania. Another song, "Mother I Sober", takes its listener along through the mind of a now adult sharing truths about childhood sexual abuse and its effects, seemingly one being a sex addiction or lust, and this is despite any outward success victims might achieve.

I include Kendrick Lamar's references, not only because I am a huge fan, but because he has given voice to his generation—to the culture, and though not the only, he's one of the most influential in recent times to give voice to the trauma and effects of childhood sexual abuse, and I commend him for it.

It's happened in my family—and it happened to me. Interestingly, I somehow thought that because I fought my offender—an uncle, away that somehow translated to not being as serious or that because I fought him away, it somehow wasn't molestation. But it was indeed molestation and it affected me.

Butch lived in the house with my aunt, grandmother and me. He wasn't there all the time, but when he was, I was afraid. I was afraid to get up in the middle of the night to go to the bathroom. I was afraid to fall asleep. When I needed to get up to go to the bathroom, he would stand in the doorway and expose his penis to me. One evening he came into the room that I shared with my grandmother, to say good night and after turning the light out, he began rubbing his hands up and down my leg. I kicked him hard. I guess being the best girl kick-ball player on the schoolyard came in handy. I yelled for my grandmother and that scared him off only until the next time. The next time he came into the bedroom where I was there playing with my hair; I don't recall where my aunt was at the time, but she wasn't at home, and my grandmother was downstairs. He came into the room wearing nothing but his boxers with his penis fully erected and exposed. I remember feeling disgusted more than afraid—by him laying his body on my bed—where he then proceeded to rub my legs. I struck him with all the force I could muster up with the rake portion of the afro-pick that I had been using to comb my hair, and he jumped up and left the room. So, here is where I share the obvious… Jesse and Dot's children were all *"fighters"*, in every sense of the word—it was instinct as well as "required" that we all knew how to defend ourselves, and I was not exempted from that. Nevertheless, I did tell my two older female cousins what he did, but I did so in a very sheepish, childlike way that I did not gain their attention or urgency about what I was saying. Fortunately, he never bothered me again. After I wrote about this in my very first book, those two cousins both came to me to apologize, stating that they did not remember, but that they were sorry. I can't begin to explain how much that mattered and meant to me because it validated my experience in that they would hear, me then even if they did not before.

The anxiety I carried because of it would show up many years later, as I parented my own children and how paranoid I was. Now sharing this for the first time…I recall my brother wresting around just roughhousing and tickling my middle daughter when she was a little girl, and I ran into the area where they were, terrified that he was "touching" her. It was perfectly innocent—an uncle playing with his niece, but I was terrified. And even still, I am not a hundred percent sure that any one of my children didn't have their own experiences in their own lives just with different characters.

LEAVING HOME

> *"Change can be scary, but it's utterly unavoidable. In fact, impermanence is the only thing you can truly rely on. If you are unwilling or unable to pivot and adapt to the incessant, fluctuating tides of life, you will not enjoy being here. Sometimes, people try to play the cards that they wish they had, instead of playing the hand they've been dealt. The capacity to adjust and improvise is arguably the single most critical human ability."*
>
> — Willard Carrol Smith

For most people leaving home usually refers to leaving their childhood home to begin an intended trajectory for college or maybe marriage but leaving home for me was about leaving a city—removing myself and my children from it. It's been many years since I left the city of Chester, Pennsylvania—and prior to that, I spent many years "trying" to leave Chester. There is a significant reason for that, I was a young girl raising a boy child and I remember there was this unction in my spirit that he would not live long if I stayed there. I was also a "reader", so other influences were at play in understanding statistics and things of that nature. However, I envisioned a city— "a vision" that depicted a state and condition of that city that was nothing like it was then but is now everything I imagined. However, I did have one benchmark and that was the murder of my oldest brother in the 70's. The older I got the more that shook me because as a little girl (before he was killed), I dreamt of someone hurting him in the streets and I jumped up from my sleep and I told my aunt—my mother's sister, who was now raising me. Nevertheless, within a week or so later, instead of sitting in her lap to tell her about my dream of someone hurting my oldest brother. Whom, I loved dearly and worshipped the ground he walked on—literally— (if his feet treaded a part of the ground, I thought that ground was sacred). I was now sitting her lap listening to her tell me that my big brother was gone which I did not understand immediately, but I understood that he would not be coming back just as my mother would not. The night before my oldest brother's death, he came to visit me at Aunt Ruth's. Squeezing his body in-between me and the tiny space at the end of the sofa where I sat with my aunt watching the

Carroll Burnett Show, he put his arms around me and asked, *"Are you okay? Is anyone hurting you?"* I responded, *"Yes, and then no."* He then looked down at the other end of the sofa where our aunt sat, obviously listening, and said to her, *"Nobody put their hands on her."* Aunt Ruth responded, *"Okay."* He then returned his attentions back to me and said, *"I love you."* He kissed me on my forehead, got up and headed for the door. I walked him to the door—watched him walk across Dewey Mann's school yard until his silhouette blended in with the night, and I could see him no more—still sadden at this memory.

I moved often—a lot and though I read this quote recently, instinctively I have always known this very thing to be true and it was a guiding principle for me throughout my erratic journey, which is another quote from Smith, *"Choosing the city you live in is as important as choosing your life partner."*

My second move to North Carolina many years later, would follow someone pulling a gun on my son. The gun pointed to his back; my son turned around facing the hoodlum that was threatening his life for what appeared to be because he wasn't from the neighborhood. My son turned to face him—and said, *"If you are going to shoot me you are going to do it with me looking at you."* I don't know what happened that the boy didn't shoot, but there was an inference that my son was recognized as a "Shaw", which actually was a big deal in that city once upon a time. Added to that, he was the star running back on the high school football team and was consistently on the front page of the local newspaper. Another thing was my niece who lived in the neighborhood seemingly had some "cred" in the neighborhood either heard or just happen to walk up on the scene and confronted the boy. Those details are vague. But he made it home alive—called me and calmly stated, *"Mom someone just pulled a gun on me."* So, this would be the manifestation of the *"unction"* I had (as a teenage mother) long before this day arrived. I don't remember anything after getting his call except, running down the hallway from my office at the University of Penn where I worked at the time, jumping in my car and it felt like I was home without ever seeing the highway. We had just moved into the home we were in, and I had some idea that the area was on the decline, but I did not imagine how drastic it was, because many years' prior this area was beautiful, a great place to raise a family where most were property owners. It was no longer that place. In fact, my father once lived there, so I was very familiar with the neighborhood. So, that night I contacted a friend that lived in Princeton, North Carolina told her what happened and pleaded that she help me find a place. Immediately she contacted someone she knew. I drove down on a Friday morning, saw the place with the owner and left him a 1500 deposit. When I returned to work on Monday, I turned in my resignation effective immediately explaining why. That evening packing began, and with some help from a neighbor—packed up a U-Haul and moved to North Carolina. I worked a temporary job while I looked to find a regular full-time one. I could not remain and risk my son becoming a statistic of gun violence, which was and has become an increased reality in that city for so many families. Though gun violence was less a threat in our new state, but it appeared, I traded into a subtler risk to my children—recalling the day my son walked into the kitchen, stood against the wall and said, *"Mom, I know you moved here because of what happened, but no one in Chester has ever offered me drugs."* With my heart racing, I responded, *"Did you take them?"* He, said, *"No."* But what was very clear as I looked at him was an unspoken message between us "this wasn't any better." What I knew was because he was being offered drugs in school with young men he had befriended—we had a problem. So that was a short-lived transition, that I don't regret. I returned to Chester city where I knew I could not stay, and did not stay, for long before I moved to a different city where I remained for many years—before deciding to take a job that meant moving to Maryland. By this time, my son was in his freshman year of college. There was plenty of in between transient activity during this phase of our lives as well, including accepting a consultant job in Georgia, and all that it entailed. But this is what I know for sure—where you live is paramount to your being, becoming, and quality of life. The preceding quote by Will Smith has been the trajectory of my life, and what I never hope to do is become lulled into a state of complacently, guised as "contentment", and lose the ability to know when it's time to pivot, even at this stage—particularly age, as a single woman. If I were to marry again, I would want my husband to have that same trait—the same gumption. But I would like to believe that at this stage of my life if I were to be married the union would have contentment and stability baked in, because marriage at this stage of life would have to be about moving forward in tandem, our individual purposes and collective support for each other.

LOVE-RELATIONSHIPS, MARRIAGE & SINGLENESS

Speaking of marriage…

One of my favorite biblical scriptures is from Psalm 27:13 KJV. "I would have fainted, unless I had believed to see the goodness of the Lord in the land of the living."

And I have. I have witnessed, experienced, live in the goodness of the Lord in real-time, so, no one can convince me otherwise. There is an expression, maybe even a song that says, "If God never does anything else for me, He's done enough." That is an absolute truth in my life. But this does not mean, I don't desire the fullness of a loving, healthy, God-guided, marital partnership.

A few years ago, April 27th, 2018, to be precise, while waiting at a mutually agreed upon welcome center location to meet up with someone that would be continuing the drive with me to our final destination. While sitting there, it was the normal rapid movement of transient people in and out. However, the woman who parked beside me was walking toward my car as I sat there waiting. I had just lowered my car window seconds prior because I started feeling a sense of being closed in. The woman looked at me and said, *"The Lord gave me a word for you, and I said, I can't say anything to her – she will think I am crazy. But the more I wrestled with it the more I heard,*

"Tell her this…" She shared that she then responded to the pressing of the Holy Spirit, saying, *"Only if her window is down when I go back, I will tell her what You say."* Now, I understand this type of thing is likely to be unique to my specific journey consequently making it difficult to reconcile for someone that is not a "Believer." Nevertheless, what the lady said next left me speechless. She said, *"You are a mighty woman of God, and He says to tell you that, "He sees you, and He heard you and because you have been faithful over little, He's about to take you into overflow. He said, the words and deeds that were spoken against you and meant to destroy you are no more. He's going to provide for you. You have been a faithful woman and a warrior"*, she said. You asked God to show himself mighty in your life… well He is about to. By this time, I was in full blown tears—but it did not end there. The lady went on to say, *"I would have imagined you to be married, but God has revealed a man in a gray suit he has a clean bald head… he's dark—very dark, and kind of tall and he's in ministry and his name is something with initials… I can't quite make them out it's R, S or T… something with initials, but this is how you will know him…* your *husband. God tells me to tell you, "You won't do this phase by yourself. He's showing me two *like* Oxen paired up and moving powerfully."* She ended with saying, *"I imagine that from your reaction that you know this to be true that it aligns with the desire of your heart."* She then prayed for me—then we prayed together and said our goodbyes.

Now before I lean in further with this story, I want to say that what I have had an opportunity to learn about prophecy has been extremely enlightening over these last few years. I have been a virtual attendee (member) of an amazing church under the teaching of a respected man of God. I won't include his details because of his renowned status, but what I will say is that in this culture of faltering ministries, and moral failure of pastors, I don't put my faith in men. But because of my relationship and study of the Word of God, I know I am currently being excellently discipled under this particular pastor's tutelage and ministry. Having said that, I understand the nuances of the scripture, "For we know in part, and we prophesy in part." [1 Corinthians 13:9 KJV]. And while this gift is real, powerful, and of great use to the ministry, it does not override our individual thoughts and impressions. So, when this prophetic message came forward, there is something worth pointing out beforehand. When the woman said, *"I would have thought you to be married…"* that was a pivotal point and likely deviation from the spiritual to the personal which supports the "in part" of the scripture concerning the prophetic gift, and that's important to note especially if you are a Believer.

I moved to Alexandria, VA in March 2019, (following a return to Pennsylvania from Maryland) after being laid off from a role that I held for just over a year. I later received a call with an offer for a job that I interviewed for previously. I eagerly headed back, started work with the company immediately, and have remained in Alexandria to-date—though not with the same company.

In May of 2019, two months into my new role as a Talent Acquisition, Recruiter we hired a new proposal writer to the organization. As customary, the Chief of Staff brought the new employee around for introductions. He had a bald head—he was dark – very dark, and kind of tall. He's wearing a gray suit, and was introduced by his initials, which overrode his actual name. From what he later shared; he was a very active member of the music ministry at his church. I asked him what his initials were short for—he told me and later reiterated that no one calls him by his full name—except for me. I never referred to him with his initials, always by his name as his initials seemed too small to suit his grand and prominent presence, and I felt warranted the full expression of his name. Now, I want to insert a bit of a transition here to share that I have written about this meeting in another book that I have now decided to not publish—at least for now anyway. I wrote the book in a true fiction format, in third person because of the details that tell more of a "love story" that are not best suited for this book. Perhaps one day I will feel the need to publish that book, but for now I do not. *This* book almost did not happen because of the struggles, conflict and contradictions, that had become my reality, thereby flying in the face of "being who I said I was."

But perhaps you have already thought as I did initially, "This is him", this is the man that the prophet spoke of. And as if that wasn't compelling enough, we were immediately fixated on each other— "enthralled" was the word he once used. There was no denying, it was palpable. And what we settled on is that it was love at first sight at the least, it was chemistry unmatched by anything I've ever experienced. The attraction between us sucked the air out of the room—it was intoxicating. So, as you can imagine, I was over the moon about our first lunch "date", still believing that "this is him", but—it was not, at least not *my* husband, I should say. And though not backing away from what we both knew was an undeniable even unexplainable attraction; he let me know during lunch that he was newly engaged. So, what I am sure of today is that he was indeed the man that was prophesized —there is no question about it. But she prophesized "in part", and where she inserted "*I would have thought you were married*" is where it became her thoughts and not what said the Lord. I know there are theories around loving someone at "first sight", but what I will say, and using some discretion, is that if I were not a believer in the concept, I am now. At some point there are certain things you get to know for yourself—no researcher, philosopher, psychologist, or theologian need tell you—because you just know it. So, what has been unearthed, as a result is the desire to have that level of love in a relationship, and a marriage in my lifetime. In my last book, I stated that "*I am content in my singleness*", (Shaw, 2020, p. 53). That contentment was greatly unraveled for a while after my meeting and interacting with the clean bald, kind of tall, very dark man in the gray suit, that goes by his initials. And while I understand that not every woman will be married, I share in the theme of transparency, that this is an unfilled area of my life because it's something that I have desired. So, while I have settled back into my "contentment" with my singleness, I am honest with myself that it's an area that I would change if I could. The difference now from times past is that I will not try to make something happen, because here's a reality for me—that never worked. But consistently, the pathology in my life, has been that everything I have *needed*, for my life, has come towards me—it has made its way to me. I never had to force, fight, or desperately seek or pursue anything that I *need*. God has pursued me throughout my entire life and provided every good and perfect gift for me, to sustain, develop, gratify, and prosper me. So, I have no reason to doubt that He knows what's best for me and will continue to provide accordingly. And like the Psalmist recorded, "I have been young, and now am old; yet have I not seen the righteous forsaken nor his seed begging bread." [Psalm 37:25 KJV], and that's a fact. Although, I have placed myself in grueling situations where I would then respond out of fear of the consequences… God never did that—what He did was covered me through those times in my life with His grace, allowing me to maintain my dignity, and enveloped me with the Love that He is, which afforded me, not only, time to grow up, but to show up as the version of myself that He always intended I'd be.

And yes, I believe in marriage. I believe that life is fuller when you are in partnership, a relationship under the covering of a healthy, purposeful marriage, and I have been reminded of that over the course of the past few years. Yes, I do navigate occasional feelings of loneliness from time to time, and it becomes more pronounced than others, especially when someone brings it to my attention. For example, like running into old school mates in a different state, many hours away from home that I'd driven to alone—consequently already feeling the loudness of my own thoughts during the five-hour ride, to then have someone ask, "Where's your husband?" And upon realization that I was by myself the expression of their surprise. Or the intrusive neighbor that asked, "Why are you by yourself? Where is your boyfriend?" Instinctively you might think he was inquiring for himself, but he is a gay man, so that was not the case. Nevertheless, I don't live in a state of obsessing over or being overwhelmed by it. In fact, I know this for sure contentment while single has many benefits.

> *"Delight yourself in the LORD, and he will give you the desires of your heart."*
>
> [Psalm 37:3 NIV]

ABOUT MY BABY BROTHER

Michael L. Shaw #9
January 7, 1967 - August 2, 2018

Now is probably a good time to share why this book is dedicated to my baby brother, Michael. When my baby brother tragically took his life, I experienced a whirlwind of emotions and physical reactions, like losing my ability to speak for an entire day—literally lost my voice, and at every attempt to speak only groans would emerge. I could not form words. My soul felt incapable of processing the reality of what I was hearing, feeling, and what I then felt was a foreseeable outcome. That "foreseeable" part is still difficult to emotionally reconcile. Recently, I watched a video clip from the actor, singer, and comedian David Mann where he spoke about his personal bout with depression and described it as "feeling that he was *drowning* and felt the only way people would understand how depressed he was would be if he completely *drowned*." That was so painful to hear because I believe that was my baby brother's resolution. So, it was at this point when I started referring to him as #9 because he was the 9th child—the baby.

Superman

Michael wore a dog tag around his neck with the Superman emblem and oftentimes T-shirts with the same. Some people thought the "S" was synonymous with his last name "Shaw", and to a degree, it was, but I knew that it was indicative of aligning himself with a form of super-natural persona—his alter ego. Recently, I started writing a piece that I have since put on hold about my fondness of superheroes and why—a fondness that I developed as a child and how it translated into an ability to tap into a higher, stronger, version of myself. I recall a time when my mom had placed me in the closet below the stairwell as punishment for doing something I had no business doing and there was a life-sized doll in there with hazel-colored eyes that glowed in the dark and I was terrified. I yelled, "*Superman, Batman, get me out of here!*" I kicked the door clean open! Well, Michael did the same to draw strength, only he did so as an adult. That emblem around his neck or on a T-shirt was not only synonymous with the "S" in his last name, but it was indicative of the strength that he had to draw on in his everyday effort to face the day—his everyday struggle to maintain the persona that we had come to know because despite the conditions passed to us both, the subsequent consequences of life choices, and the pain emotionally and physically in his case, that he had come to know as "his life." He wanted to make it. He wanted to fight it like a superhero, but he was flying without his cape. And, like every superhero—he had nemeses, but grew weary of fighting them off.

Losing my baby brother has such complexities associated with it. In fact, I am not sure that explaining or sharing those complexities as it relates to what and how I feel—not only emotionally—but spiritually and physically are within my reach to articulate. Recently, I had a dream or what felt more like a vision of him pacing back and forth in a room where it was just the two of us, but it wasn't audible—what it did seem like was a game of charades—he was messaging me, but I could not make out what he was messaging. It felt like there were questions being asked, but I could not interpret who was asking the questions as he paced back and forth giving the impression that he was not at rest, but rather still in flight. That dream or vision, as you may imagine, only exasperates the complexities of reconciling his death by suicide. For years the two of us had been estranged, and though distanced physically, emotionally, and geographically, he was not totally off my radar—but he was out of my grasp and that within the current context is a hell of a reality to have to deal with. During the days and phases of our lives prior to his marriage and relocation to Florida, he was within my grasp and during those times no particular disagreement, differences in opinions or lifestyle choices completely severed my reach or access to him. Although he was vehemently angry with me after I wrote my first book (where I asserted that our father killed our mother) so much so that it was clear that things just would not be the same between us. He was still within my reach, however and I was accessible. I never rescinded his access to me and was never going to despite the obvious issues that divided us and grew us apart. Nevertheless, following his marriage and move to Florida—we had practically become strangers to each other. In fact, it completely severed our relationship. And while I was aware of how turbulent and tumultuous his marriage, life and health had become, I settled into the reality that I had become merely just an unwelcomed bystander in the bigger scheme of his life. Nevertheless, I prayed for him diligently, nothing had changed that—nothing. During the early days of our very young lives, he was very much the protective brother and there are many stories of, not only, affection and looking out for each other that we mutually shared, but also many stories of affliction that we mutually shared as well. Nevertheless, I won't memorialize those stories here, but what I will attest to is that when we succumbed to being unapologetically prideful—the ascension towards our end—for which we were mutually culpable took root.

Nevertheless, this loss and the tragedy that played itself out literally on the virtual stage of Facebook (not the actual act) left me grappling not only, with my emotions, but also with my own mortality. While, I don't have an issue with death and dying personally. I have comfort in the transition not only from a biblical—scriptural perspective being a follower of Jesus Christ, but also from a perspective that there is no way in the world I would want to be on this side of life for an eternity. So, thank God that's not an option. However, tragic death shakes me and this one shook me to my core. Aside from the obvious of knowing and visualizing him standing there waiting and watching while a train hurled full speed towards him (if that's what really happened); I have come to an understanding as to why.

One evening as I slept perhaps dreaming at a level of being partially awake, I had what seemed like a download and revelation, and I do wish that I had awaken fully to record the actual details of the dream in the moment. But the revelation as it relates to my baby brother, #9, and his suicide has left a major wound on my soul. Losing him, aside from the obvious and apparent feelings associated with losing a sibling, specifically the youngest one, in such a tragic way scared me.

Surely, the timing of my baby brother's death following the highly publicized, high-profile celebrity coverage of Kate Spade—successful, beloved, famous, and extremely wealthy fashion icon-and then Anthony Bourdain—brilliant celebrity chef, world-travel documentarian, TV personality and author, was mere coincidence. But the timing was sequential, nevertheless. I would imagine, given the challenges that #9 was having in his personal life (marriage), financial and his intensified health challenges, the thought of suicide had entered his mind long before then—I would imagine. I would imagine that he looked for reasons to hold on just another day, a little while longer. I would imagine that some days presented him with glimpses of hope even in a dark place, and that allowed him to grab ahold of enough strength to carry on just another day… but I do imagine that even still the pain, rejection, disappointment, and façade of a life being fully lived but barely lived, became too much to continue. I would imagine. I do not know how his physical and emotional pain co-existed in tandem with each other—if one perpetuated the other—if one did not exist would the other, but nevertheless, I don't know, and I won't know. But what I do know is that I was encouraged by his "seeming" strength and resilience in the face of such overwhelming challenges. So, while our relationship was estranged on and off again, I could peek into his day-to-day life via social media. It was through this medium I was able to at least "check on him." This allowed me enough visibility to know that he was functioning, and that he was holding on and showing up for his life, per se. In fact, just the day before his post stating he was taking his life, he shared a post of a boxing video he had watched online and the day prior, a funny post or comment about where turkey bacon came from. So, the contrast from one day to the next was seemingly extreme, but it wasn't extreme at all. Social media presents us with illusions, and in some cases deceptive imagery, abstract and intentional depictions of a life lived one way that may otherwise be something altogether different. Nevertheless, because there were days that I was experiencing my own turmoil, I was encouraged to keep pressing, to keep moving, to keep showing up because— "if he could do it, so could I." This may fly in the face of my unrelenting spiritual "strength" and professed faith, but the reality is my brother's resilience was inspiration for me and he didn't know it. But when he committed suicide, I was shaken by the reality of what he had done. I had become keenly aware of how fragile I was in that moment, because of the times past when suicide had crossed my mind. When #9 took his life, I found myself grabbling with my own frailties because contrary to "looked" different, that is what looked like progress and a successful trajectory and was different from my baby brother's outcomes, at the root a truth existed that our outcomes really weren't that different. I always felt we were two sides of the same coin. We were similar in age—the products of the same familial brokenness—the seemingly *"cursed" conditions* that preceded our outcomes, with the difference being that I was "raised" and "parented" in those critical seven developmental years. Michael on the other hand basically raised himself. Our father provided him with the basics of shelter and food, but he was left to figure the rest out on his own—he modeled our dad in that process, and because our father gave him permission to drop out of school in the 9th grade, I believe the consequences of that is, he was never able to have or maintain a financial trajectory that would have afforded him a sustainable quality of life. What's even more tragic about this is that he was super smart, and though his Facebook posts were often flawed and poorly written, they were in no way an indication of his intellectual capabilities. I remember sitting at the table in tears trying to do my homework, an algebra problem, and he was on the other side of the room and saying, "Read it to me." I did, and he gave me the answer—just like that. That depth of him would never be realized or maximized because his education was thwarted. On the other hand, within those critical seven years, I (not nearly as smart as Michael), was not allowed to miss a day of school unless I was near death—the only exception being the day my cycle started at age ten, and for me that was comparable to feeling like I was having a near death experience. Additionally, I mimicked my aunt—a professional woman—in food services (by way of Aramark at Cheyney University), a historically Black University in Cheyney, Pennsylvania—who also did staff work. I remember watching her sitting on the sofa processing payroll manually on an accounting paper— it would be in her lap sprawling downward on the floor. There was a day when she took me to work with her and I got to see her in action. Something I never forgot was her giving her boss "the business" for something she disagreed with that he did or said—it was clear who the boss really was that day. It left a huge impression on me.

I recall a time sitting at the dining room table where I was supposed to be doing my homework—flipping the pages in my workbook pretending that I was doing payroll. So, when I received my first W-2 professional job offer from Commonwealth Land Title in Center City Philadelphia as an administrative assistant (although I had many odd jobs prior to this one) this was a "real" job, so I excitedly made my way to the house on 2022 West 4th street to tell my aunt the good news. By this time, I had graduated high school despite having my son at age seventeen. I also attended a local trade program that offered administrative-clerical certificates. Additionally, I went to what was known at that time as American Business Institute (ABI), a sham of a business school that was milking the Financial Aid process. But I did gain valuable workplace decorum there. That day, my aunt who in my opinion was a stoic, no nonsense kind of woman, went upstairs and came down with two leather work bags and handed them to me—one brown and the other black she said, "Take these you can have them for your new job." She never cracked a smile, but I knew for a fact that she was pleased and probably even proud of me—and this was a gesture of that. It was by far one of the happiest days of my life because, like what Michael craved from our father; I craved from my aunt Ruth, and that was her approval. I carried those bags faithfully until they were completely worn out. But as Kate Spade's, Anthony Bourdain's —and so many others since, of whose deaths by suicide would attest, achievement, and success have no power over thoughts and acts of suicide and depression. For this reason, I found myself now chasing life, trying to find retreat from the heaviness of survivor's guilt concerning Michael.

So, my challenge today is to move beyond just showing up for my life, but to show up for life as a whole… not just my individual life, the concept of "life." I see the devastation that my baby brother's suicide has caused his children and grandchildren, and the processing of this will extend far beyond today's calendar. The processing and healing from this will be far-reaching like a ball of yarn being unraveled. So, it's seeing this in real-time that gives me some perspective. And though I believe in the theory, that publicized and other means of perpetuating and stirring up thoughts of suicide may possibly lead someone to carry out the actual action, this makes me think of when it was rumored that the late Phyllis Hyman had committed suicide and she had not. She appeared on a local radio platform to refute the ridiculousness of the rumors, but one month later—she committed suicide. I also believe that contemplating the devastation left behind for those that we love is also a viable deterrent. Then there's the influence of the Word of God—biblical principles and ideology that I believe are sustainable influences on one's ability to keep pressing, but I am not professing that it negates the possibility because I don't believe that is a fair assertion to make; especially since there are reports of several preachers and/or ministers who have committed suicide in recent years. And social media does not help.

So, as it relates to the death by suicide of my baby brother, when a loved-one, especially a sibling commits suicide, it's like a punch in the stomach, perhaps even repeated punches, and when those metaphorical punches are landed at the hands of a strong, skilled "fighter", they tend to be especially devastating blows... so much so that your own life flashes before you—you even try escaping because the pain is so unbearable. I also realize that this punch or punches to the stomach are internalized and personalized for each loved-one that's left with the transfer of pain from the victim to the *victims* because with that punch seems to come a haunting personalized message that says, "This is for you not helping me, this one is for the days I needed help and you couldn't help. This one is especially for you, for that time I cried out and you did not hear me. So, *you* take this pain... and *you* deal with it. I have tried to parlay this revelation into anger, so that I could be mad at him for committing suicide (selfishly) thinking it would help the pain to subside, but just like I could never stay mad at him in life, I can't do it in death either because the reality is we were both like two toddlers wobbling and trying to walk for many years. That's where we had very similar struggles navigating an interrupted childhood, which led into a disjointed adulthood. The difference in outcomes would have everything to do with those critical seven years following my mom's death, and how differently they were cultivated—it's a truth that can't be denied. Even with my faltering all through and in-between time, there was a foundation that I continued to reach from despite the rocky roads getting there. My aunt said a couple of profound things to me as she stood in the vestibule as I made my exit from the only home I had known for those seven years: "*You know right from wrong.*" In its simplicity, it was a jolt to my consciousness that I could not escape, and for many years following walking out that door, I vacillated *knowing right from wrong* was a truth to be reckoned with.

Once on my own at that very young age, admittedly, I struggled a great deal with my identity in terms of who I was alongside my siblings. This was mostly attributed to what I felt as "being different" when I was around them.

My aunt knew too that I would because she also said that as she walked me to the door. Nevertheless, I am now affirmed that "All things work together for those who love the Lord"—*all things.*

MICHAEL WORSHIPED HIM

I loved my father, but Michael worshipped him. The love I held for my father is very descriptive in nature and seemingly very intuitive too. My father to me was as physically beautiful of a Black man, I had witnessed, and still today that holds true to me. He was sculpted physically and graced with a physique that remained consistent as if it was hand carved. He flashed a smile that literally flashed with a gold crown, making him appear all the grander. His walk was my first assessment of what poetry in motion must have looked like and his voice was as unique as all of the rest of him—a fast, rapid linguistic in a deep monotone traced with a seriousness and always, in my opinion, having some degree of urgency to it. But when I think about my father's voice; I never heard it as often as I would have liked to. In my time with him he did not talk much, but when he did it was true to forum, deep monotone, fast, rapid, serious, and urgent. The other thing, I think very important was that when he spoke it was with a deep sense of wisdom that I felt from him. His words, to me, carried power and evoked a sense of teaching. But despite what I interpret as the seriousness and importance of his voice; I believe that all my siblings, at some point or another, have mimicked his voice giving us all a good laugh.

Nevertheless, my father and I had our moments of intense contention, but nothing changed my love for him. I recall an incident when I was staying with him while carrying my son. I was in the habit of preparing my meals for the week and I was cooking a pot of collard greens to ensure adequate vegetable consumption because (I was super careful about my nutrition during this pregnancy). I cooked in my long white robe covered in a pink floral design, with a beautiful pink ribbon, serving as a belt tied neatly in a bow—a gift given to me from my aunt Ruth. I made several trips from the bedroom to the kitchen to check on the pot of greens I was preparing, and more than once my father said, "*Put on some clothes.*" It was hindsight, but I wondered if the pronounced visual of my pregnancy unsettled him. Nevertheless, I replied, "*I will when I am done.*" My final trip from the bedroom to the kitchen still in my long white robe, resulted in my father jumping up from his recliner, and accosting me, repeating, "*Put some clothes on!*" Though extremely angry, I said nothing after he released me from his grip. I continued into the kitchen, only this time removing the simmering pot of collard greens, returned to the living room, and threw them on him. Jumping up from the recliner where he sat, he yelped and yelled, "*You are just like your mother!*" I learned from that statement more than he may have realized he was sharing. Nevertheless, and perhaps a bit of a paradox, there was still something about my father that made me feel safe even when I did not fully understand what that meant. He had a persona that some say qualified him as a "G", which in the culture is indicative of being a "gangsta", grand, well-dressed, having financial means, endeared, and having "swag" all of which I believe applied to my father. He drove Cadillacs, toted a gun, nails were manicured, and he was impeccably dressed with a sense of style that has truly been passed down through my family amongst the men, especially Michael. And I can certainly understand how he and a woman (girl) who in her own right was a beautiful, stylish, and a captivating sight to see, would find themselves connected.

Little has been recorded and shared (if known) about my father's pilgrimage from his roots in Orangeburg, South Carolina to the city of Chester, Pennsylvania. The research that I am currently conducting to gain further insight into his journey is a work in progress and a very daunting process indeed. However, what I have discovered is that there was (is) a "Shaw" plantation in Orangeburg, South Carolina - Williamsburg County to which there may very well be a connection to his last name. Nevertheless, there is a great deal of intrigue around his ancestry and pilgrimage prior to Orangeburg, SC that could possibly explain so much about his physical and inherent characteristics. What is clear is that my father's journey from the Carolina's to the city of Chester, PA surely had a significant influence on the boy he was and the man he became, the life of Jesse LeGrande Shaw did not just begin with the father we came to know or didn't know for that matter. His middle name alone speaks volumes to what we *don't* know. That said, my current research is bending strongly towards the possibility that his origin is of Haitian decent. This would indeed explain his middle name as well as mine, Yevette (which is misspelled) or at least spelled as an English variation of what was surely intended to be the French version of the name. That is supported by the fact that my oldest brother's middle name was Francis and my older sister's middle name was Jean all of which were names appointed by my father. All the other middle names subscribed to my siblings were clearly given by my mother as they were given middle names like, Victoria, Leroy and names of her mother and siblings, e.g., Elsie, Lafenus, Lankford, etc.

One of the things that I learned about my father from our own personal interaction was that he was smart. One of a few examples that spoke to that, was once while reading an article and stumped by the meaning of a word, he told me what it meant even though I had mispronounced it. He read the paper often, which to some may not be a big deal, but I always found it impressive—perhaps because I observed him to get to know him. In fact, he's why I started reading the newspaper. Another day he left me a note written on a brown colored paper napkin and to this day, I wish I had that napkin. Oh, how I wished I had saved it. His handwriting was impeccable (cursive) something we see rarely anymore. It was scripted so beautifully and his choice of words on that napkin were so carefully chosen. I remember thinking, "*Wow, my dad is really smart.*" I remember that, and it was then that I thought my love for writing and my relationship with words may have come from my father, but I am not blessed with his penmanship.

Another fond memory of my father was his being front and center at my high school graduation—he was there with my baby brother and that made it one of the proudest moments of my life. There was also a time in the 70s when Hess gas station featured "dolls from around the world" that anyone who purchased a full tank of gas would receive and my father would bring me one of those dolls every week. He also bought me my first clarinet, and organ, both of which were fleeting interests. But the most significant purchase he made for me was an umbrella. It was a purple umbrella with a mahogany handle that he had engraved. I was a young girl (deemed adult) living on my own as a single parent, and I did not have a car. Consequently, I walked everywhere and because he was observant of that, he bought me that umbrella when he purchased jewelry for my sisters that Christmas. It remains (though long gone) as one of the most precious gifts I had received.

My father came to the city of Chester from Orangeburg, SC and resided with his uncle Booker Shaw under the guise or just blended in as a son instead of a nephew. From a very early age my father acquired work as a steel worker-laborer via Baldt & Anchor. So, whenever I am at a waterfront or enjoying the experience of boating, I find myself experiencing a nostalgic moment when seeing the bolts & anchors that are used to keep boats docked as I think, "My father's hands may have touched (welded) these." Baldt & Anchor founded by Frederick Baldt [1841-1916]. "The Company was formed to "manufacture, buy, sell, and deal with steel or iron or both and all like or kindred products". Their first product was the "Baldt Patent Stockless Anchor" patented by Frederick

Baldt, October 27, 1896. Anchors were produced by the Penn Steel Castings Company" (Perry, 1993). My father made a decent living here and as far as I know it's the only actual job he held—starting as a young boy, shortly after the time of his arrival from SC to PA. I can attest, having seen one of his paystubs one day, that his earnings were impressive for that era. So, amongst other things, I think it's safe to say that he ended up in Pennsylvania by way of the Carolinas because of work in the booming steel industry at that time.

My father did not live too long beyond his retirement. I am not sure of the exact timing, but his retirement from work that he did basically all his life from a boy through his early 60s was met with a diagnosis of cancer seemingly of the lungs, and if I remember correctly, traveled upwards to his brain. This was a hard reality for me and certainly for other siblings as well, especially my baby brother who went to live with our father after my mother's death. I imagine that it was significantly hard for my oldest two living brothers too as they were extremely close.

During the time of my father's failing health in the late 80's, I had gone to live with his sister in Dudley, NC in an attempt to make a better life for me and my son. As stated before, there was always something about living in the city of Chester that never felt welcoming or safe to me. I found myself in constant flight in my attempts to escape that city. Nevertheless, upon the news of his failing health and diagnoses of which I am confident he knew of when I left, is why he was so adamant and eagerly supportive of me leaving. In addition, I think he was pleased I was going to be with *his* sister, which I believe he felt was a sort of recompense to his legacy because up until that point my upbringing and parental influences were that of my mother's sister who raised me after her death. Although, I am extremely grateful that I was raised by my mother's sister, I do know it created some tension, not only for me, but for my father concerning my "identity" per se.

My dad passed away shortly after my return, and I visited him every day until then. On that day, when my baby brother arrived to see our father, he received the news that our dad was gone. He just took off running… he ran all the way across the neighboring school yard until he was no longer in eyesight. That visual tore me to pieces because it was so remanence of my oldest brother's departure across a school yard all those many years prior. It still hurts because Michael seemingly had been running ever since that day—until he committed suicide.

> *Every so often I check in with that seven-year-old girl standing there on that cemetery ground and remind her — "His promise is still true — it still stands, He is still taking care of you." That promise is irrevocable.*

🌷 Your Thoughts…

_____
_____
_____
_____
_____
_____
_____
_____
_____
_____
_____
_____
_____
_____
_____
_____

Chapter 2
WE ARE HERE NOW

So, when considering my earlier start in life, I have many things to be proud of, grateful for and could not have done without God's grace, care, and love towards me. I have obtained college degrees alongside my children. I have a substantial career in Human Resources. I am a founder of a NPO, a published author, and mother to three amazing humans and grandmother to one. So as previously stated, if God does nothing else for me, He has done enough.

So, I reiterate that we must show up for our own lives. It's no one else's responsibility to do so and showing up for your own life vs me showing up for mine looks different, and I imagine it feels differently too, especially when the influence and influx of social media holds one's focus captive. The addictive allure of social media, feeding and altering of one's psyche certainly can make it hard for some to focus on their own realities. In fact, I would venture to say that the diversion to social media oftentimes aids in the anesthetizing of one's own realities. Consequently, making it even more difficult to galvanize the necessary tenacity, grit, and attention required to show up fully for one's own life. It makes the endeavor of making your impact in life tenuous at best because you aren't giving the focus and energy that is being absorbed by watching someone else's via a vehicle of illusion such as Facebook for example.

Yet we desire to be more, do more, to "level up", and have more of an impact on life. I don't believe anyone innately wants to be stagnated, mediocre, depleted or defeated—but unless we apply focus, create the space to be and to become, unless we ascribe our lives to the narrative and behaviors that will produce our desired end, we will not be who we say we want to be—doing what we say we want to do.

Described in the preceding book, "Becoming The Person You Told People You Were", the person you "told people you were" isn't necessarily a verbal or audible proclamation, but one that you intrinsically are, and though the outward realization may not yet be, it's there— it's in you to bring forth.

So, despite what may have happened to any of us in the past, despite any poor decisions or behaviors we may have engaged in because of those conditions—we are not relegated to any lower version of ourselves, and therefore can commit to better outcomes. So, my challenge for all of us is to set boundaries around energy, focus, and discipline detractors, including people. It's critical to your process of being and becoming who you say you are even if it's not visible right now.

As a tenured Human Resources professional with a few of decades of experience, I have witnessed the ebbs and flows of industry and culture. And one of the many changes that I have witnessed is a shift from what was once deemed a best practice, is "excellence" albeit in your work, career, community, and relationships.

Recently, my twenty-five-year-old daughter said to me, "You have that old person's mentality, getting up and starting work at 7:00 in the morning." I responded, "I most certainly do. Odd to you because your generation is lazy." Now somewhere in-between both of those assertions, lies the truth. The conversation really is about a generational or culture-shift, and certainly not about anyone being lazy or not. But there is no denying that the sense of extreme individualism is eating away at the ideals that we all have a part to play in the larger scheme of life's eco-system —we are becoming a very 'me myself and I' culture.

Chapter 3
HOME*LESS*

"When I think of home, I think of a resting place, a place where there's peace quiet and serenity... I wish I were home; I wish I were back there with the things I've been knowing. Maybe there is a chance for me to go back now that I've had some direction... And maybe I can convince time to slow up, giving me enough time in my life to grow up... time be my friend and let me start again... I have had my mind spun around in space, but I've watched it growing... If you are listening to God please don't make it hard to know if we [I] should believe the things that we [I] see, just should we [I] try and stay or should we [I] just run away, or would it be better to just let them be ..."

The preceding selected lyrics from the song "Home" written by Charlie Smalls, but made famous by the incomparable songstress, Stephanie Mills has been a background theme song I think in so many people's lives for several generations, and definitely in mine. I used to cry when I heard it as a child watching the Wizard of OZ. But recently, when I heard it—it impacted me as if a culmination to my life's story and trajectory.

Previously mentioned, I moved to Alexandria, Virginia in March 2019, after moving back to Pennsylvania from Maryland following a layoff from my job at that time. But what I did not include there intentionally was that in-between Maryland and Pennsylvania was Canada. I had the support of my daughters in terms of its necessity and/or it being a good idea following all that was happening with me emotionally—job loss, subsequent necessity to move, my brother's suicide was a lot and taking its toll. So, I left for Canada with a plan, but before being able to make it to Canada I was held up in Portland Maine for at least a week due to turbulence on the waters that would not allow for the trip to continue which consequently led to other transport issues. Once the time came where I could finally get over to Canada to the beautiful B&B in Nova Scotia where I reserved an extended stay while I figured out the "what's next" phase. As you may know you can stay in Canada for up to six months as a non-resident, but not beyond that. What I later learned that many people navigated between Portland Maine, and Canada. So, I secured a semi-furnished apartment in Portland, Maine with the intent of doing the same while I worked through the bureaucracy of trying to get Canadian citizenship. That's what I wanted to do but I would end up falling in love with Maine—until the day loneliness and being alone hit me like a ton of bricks! I would awaken one morning thinking; I need to go home!" But I had no home to go to, but I knew that I was no match for the loneliness that was starting to suffocate me—to *drown* me. Also, my class reunion was coming up that November, and I had already determined that I was not missing it that year, so if for no other reason, I was coming back for the reunion, and so I did. But when I hit New York, hell broke loose, or should I say snow broke loose. I spent 12 hours stuck on the expressway in a snowstorm like none I have ever experienced in recent years—slipping, sliding, stuck, with every type of vehicle—sandwiched in between oversized trucks and sixteen wheelers. I was definitely afraid that I would not make it safely, but I did make it safely, and never returned back to Portland, Maine.

But the other reality was that I was homeless once back in Pennsylvania. I stayed where I could. I couch-surfed between my two daughter's homes, but in no way was that sustainable, and it was a dreadful feeling of not only being displaced but being in the way. And despite their love for me, I was in the way. Shortly thereafter, my stipend that I was living off had run out. So, I was not only without housing—but I was also without out income—it was a terrifying time. Between my three children (largely my son), and a few friends, I don't even want to imagine how much worst things could have gotten.

And then seemingly out of nowhere, I got a call about a job that I had interviewed for—and then an offer. The job was in Annandale, Virginia, and I would initially have to navigate housing arrangements by way of Airbnb, and house shares for a while until I secured my current condo. And because I am sharing this extensive detail to weave together the larger picture of no matter how many messes, bad decisions, and missteps I have made in my "need" to protect, defend, take care of myself; God has absolutely taken care of me, provided for me, and literally made available every single thing for me that I have needed when it was clear that I could not have possibly done it myself.

Eventually, I would leave that job to begin working for wonderful non-profit until the Covid:19 pandemic broke out and job losses occurred. So, like so many, I was laid off again, and after hundreds of applications and no offers; I had become convinced that I would probably never find a job, but I still prayed diligently asking that God open a door because simultaneously another reality that was unfolding was the house share that I was in was becoming an unhealthy—and unsafe environment. And again, true to form, God answered. This particular morning there was an email from a job-board site, asking that I respond to the email, and so I did. This was not a job that I applied for. I interviewed over the phone, 2 days later was asked to do a second interview with a different person, and the following day I received an offer for a job that I did not apply for and yet nothing from those that I did. A few months after realizing that I may have a career with this organization, I started thinking about the next critical step which was moving.

I remember the day I heard, *"Go over there."* I was

picking up a grilled chicken Caesar salad from a nearby restaurant. I remember thinking, "I don't know what's over there." And approximately three days later I heard again, "Go over there." This was while coming past from work, so I went to the home I was living in, changed into my workout clothes, and headed back over to this location. The place where I found myself is a lovely, tree-lined condominium community, and as I stood there at the entrances corner, I hear "look up." So, I looked up at the units that my back was initially facing—simultaneously putting the address in the google machine to learn that it was available. So, make a long story shorter, I now live in this beautiful condominium that I love more than any home I have ever lived in. And once upon a time, I would have never thought, wanted, or even claim to have wanted to live in Virginia because Maryland, specifically the Bowie, Crofton areas are my preferred places of residence, and I was fixated on returning back there, but God in all of His magnificent glory, sovereignty, and care for me met me where I was and provided for me there. Jokingly, I say to people, I live close enough to Maryland to see it from my window if my windows were not surrounded with the beautiful pines that provide me with the most spectacular view from my third-floor condo.

"I will take care of you."

—God

Chapter 4
HIGHER VERSION OF SELF

In 2022 I released "Becoming The Person You Told People You Were," published by Christian Faith Publishers—in- tended to be inspiration for those that read it, and though so much of the feedback was extremely positive, and encouraging, there was one critique, that, *"It was not de- tailed enough about your personal life, and your struggles. I wanted to know more about what you have been through, so I was disappointed."* Aside from sharing with this reader that those details were shared in older books, I thought in that moment, there will always be someone that wants to confine you to your past—some people prefer to see you through the lens of who or where you use to be. Now, I am in no way saying this was the case of this particular person. In fact, I am confident they just wanted a full view of the arc—the history and background that preceded and perpetuates my perspective today, and that's fair. But what I hope everyone takes away from this book is that no matter where you are in life, even in this very moment—there is a future version of you, and that's the person that needs your energy, focus, and commitment, that's the person you are on this journey to meet. He or she is the legacy you want to leave behind. I fully understand the role that one's past plays in their shaping of who they are in the current moment, but to focus on one's past, to regurgitate it repeatedly to frame or justify one's current status is a recipe for stagnation, and mediocracy.

There is a biblical scripture that I love, *"Forget the former things; do not dwell on the past."* (NIV), and the KJV, language reads, *"Remember ye not the former things, nor consider the things of old."* So, while I do acknowledge the influence of my past on my life today, I have chosen to grow beyond it so I can reach forward, create fresh new vision and ideas for a life that is lived well.

For so many years of my life I framed my life's narrative around my past as if to find cause, justification or blame for what I felt to be a lack of required support that I needed to be safe, successful, and whole.

But as I committed to renewing my thoughts, I began living better. And life simultaneously presented me with resources, jobs, books, courses, education, new and different people, new and different states, countries, and it was those influences that began shaping, reframing, and cultivating the person that I am on this journey to be today. As long as my narrative was centered in my past there remained the conflict—this push and pull of pretending to be who I wanted to be vs. actually being and becoming who I wanted to become. The disadvantage of holding on to the bad hand of cards that I was dealt is that my heart and mind wasn't open to receive a better hand to be dealt for the next phase of my life.

So, yes, I am indeed one of nine children from my mother, and one of 10 from my father. Losing my mother at seven-years-of age, and basically being on my own at fourteen or fifteen, and then pregnant by sixteen; absolutely bore its consequences but with each new day came a new opportunity towards a different outcome—a new narrative, and that's my current reality. And yes, I have experienced encounters with people, family, and a couple of friends that were uncomfortable seeing me through that lens because seeing me only through the lens of my past challenges made them feel familiar or in common with me—I have reconciled that this is not my issue to contend with—it's theirs. And I write this to say, the same applies to anyone that finds themselves in that awkward space. You are not required to accommodate by reverting to a narrative that no longer serves you and the higher version of yourself.

One of the reasons I never found comfort or stability in the homes of other family members after leaving my aunt's home (my home) was because I was caught between two identities. The foundation that was laid there in those seven years and then that to which I was abruptly being introduced, all the while still a child, left me vacillating, and navigating, a grown-up lifestyle that felt like trying to swim without water, and dancing without feet. I was pretending to be. I was pretending to be okay, courageous, and stable. I was pretending to be whole; I was pretending to be smart, and knowledgeable. I was pretending to be an adult. In fact, I pretended at that for so long that I didn't notice when the lines got blurred. But amid it all, I had a sensing that I was more than my circumstances, and innately sensed that pretending to be courageous, successful, stable, okay, and productive was an internal GPS taking me towards its truth, and I would eventually meet up with that woman—that version of myself. And I don't know how my life would have turned out or the path I would have ventured to take had those critical seven years not been guided by the principles and tutelage of my aunt, grandmother, cousins, and uncle "Duck", all whom became my village at that house during those seven years, but one thing I am certain of is that it would have been different—how so, I don't know—but definitely different.

Of my ten siblings, five are still living. Michael's suicide in 2020 remains such a sad reality for many reasons, of which is that he never got to meet his future self, and nor did his children and grandchildren. He didn't get to witness or give his youngest—first to be married, daughter away; nor the amazing live at-home birthing of her first child. So that's the tension with suicide it seems because the decision is made in a moment that seems unsurmountable therefore denying yourself, and those that love you an opportunity to share in the fullness of your fully manifested self. And as stated previously, in no way am I attempting to minimize the depth of pain or mental complexities that can bring someone to this decision because I have felt it before; I know how it feels. However, hope prevailed, and God only knows how deeply, I wanted the same for Michael.

Chapter 5
UN-STUCK

So, while hanging out in Nova Scotia, Canada, that much-needed respite following being laid off from my job shortly after moving into my new residence, immediately followed by the traumatic loss of my baby brother, I stopped in a little bookstore that had a flashing "CLEARANCE SALE" sign across the window. And what seemed to be an aimless pursuit of looking through a pile of used books, turned out to be that "thing" — that repeated, consistent, unexplainable, yet just for me purposed thing that happens for my life's sake all the time. I was drawn to the title, "Getting Unstuck" a book by Timothy Butler published via Harvard Business Review Press, (2007). I immediately concluded, because it was a HBR publication that it was business related only, though the "stuck" I was feeling in that moment was emotional pain, I could also relate to the business/career version of it. So, I purchased the book and found myself completely enthralled—pulled in from the very first quote, "The way up and the way down are one in the same, —Heraclitus" (Butler, T., 2007).

What I would discover throughout the pages of this book is, yes, I was "feeling" stuck and that it hadn't started at the loss of my brother, but his sudden death was the point where the reality had arrived that nothing else could be added onto my soul or I'd come undone.

I don't know this at all to be true, but if I were to guess, I'd guess that Mr. Butler was a Believer because the tone of his writing was laced with grace, compassion, and empathy and not the self-aggrandizement that I have experienced with this niche of publication. And though the author wrote through a lens of psychology and philosophy which happens to be my love-languages, he managed to do so at a pedestrian level.

So, one of the things I hope to have as a takeaway for you as a reader is to examine how the Covid:19 Pandemic has unearthed and reshaped the ideas of what really matters in life. So many people lost jobs, and others left jobs. And albeit lost or left, many have not returned to "work." As an Industrial Psychology and Human Resources professional, I naturally want to know what ignited this "great resignation." There are various reasons to speak to, but the most common response (aside from childcare), has been "purpose." People are and have discovered that when the world literally was put on lockdown, that they wanted more meaningful lives, "purpose-driven lives", and roles that made a difference in the lives of humanity, not just padding the pockets of shareholders and demands on their time and lives that did not fulfill them or their creativity.

In the throes of a global pandemic, people were starting to contemplate becoming "unstuck." I was one of those people. And though I was in no position to not return to work when an opportunity presented itself, but I understood the plight of those that did not. As the creative that I am, I relate to those that felt compelled to plow a new path for their lives—to seize the time they had on their hands to dare create something new that would fill them with passion, purpose, vision, and joy. During the height of a once in a hundred-year pandemic, people discovered "who they wanted to be" and for many of them it meant taking on a trajectory that looked like a downward transition yet proved to be the most rewarding thing they've done in their lives—people were afforded an opportunity to revisit, and reevaluate the question, "*What do you want to be when you grow up?*"

Recently, I caught up with an old coworker. He has a tremendous career trajectory and makes half million a year easy. His statement that, "*This is not what I want my life to be. Yes, we have to eat, but I am not making the impact that I want to make in life. I want to build a NPO to help develop children*" echoes the sentiments of so many people post pandemic introspection.

And this is just one of many stories I have listened to and read that supports the truth that "we are all spiritual" even if we don't give voice to it through any specific religious doctrine. Something that can't be measured or quantified compels a man that doesn't memorialize or compartmentalize his spiritual inclinations, to want to give of his gifts, talents, and means to help others, when he could otherwise just go on and live his life as is. But as he states, "*This is not what I want my life to be.*" Why? Because intrinsically, he understands the significance of the quote from Heraclitus.

Jesus washing his disciples' feet is not just some "story" it's at the heart of our humanity. It's who and why we are. I admire anyone that washes someone's feet because it's not the most glamorous, or exhilarating of tasks, but it is humbling for both the giver and the receiver, and a vivid example of how we are to respect, serve, and care for each other. And if any of us are fortunate enough to be able to give—give. If you are able to reach for someone—reach. If you have a gift or resources use them to serve others.

> "*The way up and the way down are one in the same,*
>
> —Heraclitus

> "… Whosoever exalts himself will be humbled, and whoever humbles himself will be exalted."
>
> —Matthew 23:12 KJV

Chapter 6
DO WHAT YOU SAY YOU DO

There's another favorite and guiding biblical scripture that reads, "Call those things which be not as though they were" from the KJV of the Bible. The NIV version reads, "God who gives life to the dead and calls into being things that were not." [Romans 4:17]

During a short stint of marriage, my then husband, had a young daughter and what I remember most about her was her adamant assertions about who she was—not who she wanted to be—not what she'd hope to do. She unequivocally stated, "I am this thing or the other and will do this, and I will have this by this time, and there were no visible realities that seemingly supported those outcomes." But today, as far as I know, and based on my last interaction with her as an adult, she is precisely doing the thing with her career and life just as she stated when she was a child and is exactly who she said she'd be.

So, when the Word of God speaks of calling those

things that are not as though they were —that's what it looks like, which by the way has nothing to do with being Christian or not. This is another example of what it is to be spiritual whether we articulate it as such or not. Words carry life, they create life, they evolve albeit rightly or wrongly—words evolve and create life outcomes.

Dr. Maya Angelo put her spin on the biblical scriptures when she penned "Words are things", and I agree with Dr. Angelou that, "One day they'll be able to measure the power of words." But until then, they can be qualified by the numerous life stories that mirror the words or personal prophecies that have been spoken about or over them. So, say only what you want to produce in and for your life and leave the rest unsaid—unthought.

I have also come to understand the power of image and vision. I was never one to create 'Vision Boards", but I have witnessed the usefulness of them in the lives of people I know and love. My daughter for instance, at a point in her life had no outward experiences that would lend itself to the realities that would soon be true in her life. I recall her showing me her vision board during that time—a time when life was really dealing her a bad hand of proverbial cards. And then I remember the day when one thing after another that were once mere pictures on an oversized piece of construction paper, began to show up as a result of her courage, resilience, grit, focus, determination, patience, and service. She worked hard and persisted with the images in mind. So today, I have added that feature to my toolbox as well, and it has proven to have merit.

Even writing this very book required that I keep the

mission and vision in front of me, so that I stay on track to get it done because otherwise I am not so sure that I would have gotten it done —at least not this year. On my writing desk in my bedroom sits a small easel board with messaging written all over it to remind, inspire, and focus me on doing what I know I need to do, but more importantly what I "say I do." It has become very easy to make posts on social media that project a persona of who and what we say we are and do, and yet not be doing it at all. As stated in "Becoming The Person You Told People You Were", *"It's a thin line: this is not the same as pretending to be something that you are not and lying about who you are to yourself and to others for the sake of appearances"* (Shaw, 2020, pg. 20). But for the most part, it's not intentional to be disingenuous, but because it's easy to get off track—to get distracted and deflated by the influence of everything else around us including the use of social media. But more than anything else, it's critical to be true to yourself, honest with yourself. If you project that you are something or someone that does something meaningful and of substance, it's probably a good idea that you do and be what you say.

Make you and your life your priority. Working for someone else and furthering someone else's agenda, or their vision is likely a reality that can't be avoided for most of us, but it should not consume our lives and divert us from carving out and executing our own agendas—our own visions. Being ushered into the corporate or industrial arena to support ourselves, to pay bills is a thing; I can't refute that. But if this global pandemic has pulled back the curtain on anything, it has revealed that people want more out of their lives in terms of substance, contribution, and impact that outlives our mortality. This is the truth that lies in-between the ideas about work that I have vs. the ideas about work that my twenty-five-year-old has. The pendulum no longer swings extreme left or right leaving no room for self-discovery, and creativity, and people are rethinking and recalibrating their lives accordingly.

I would be willing to propose a challenge that for anyone seeking to live out their purpose, gifting, or calling or to even discover what that is, that if daily introspection, meditation, diligent and consistent prayer be made a priority, you'll discover what that contribution or impact should and could be.

> *"His divine power has given us everything we need for this life and godliness through the full knowledge of the One who called us by His own glory and excellence."*
>
> 2 Peter 1:3 NIV

Chapter 7
GIFTS, TALENTS & THINGS

In 2003-04, I wrote a book titled the same as this chapter's title, and though I did have it printed with a local commercial printer; I did not promote it because I never officially independently published it. However, from that book there was a chapter titled, "*What's Praise and Prayer Got to Do With it*?" The "it" that I referred to is the "gift", our gifts, talents—that thing that brings you a sense of purpose and value. That thing that you think you may have been born to do, but it feels vague in most instances, and that's when praise and prayer comes in. Prayer, meditation, praise also shown in verbal expressions of gratitude and gratefulness clears out the junk of distraction and pushes out the voices of doubt, rejection, depression, and all other forms of discouragement. My experience with people is they view through the lens of only being capable of being or doing one thing, at a time, and that's just not true. So, a corporate executive can own a catering business, a human resources manager can be a founder of their own non-profit, a team lead can be a jazz musician, a corporate finance officer, can be a social media influencer, YouTuber, and podcaster.

One day while speaking to a caller about the establishment of my non-profit, she mentioned that she discovered that I was also a published author while looking me up online. She asked me, "How do you find the time for all of this?" I jokingly responded, "If I stop to think about it, it may scare me, so I just do it", but there may have been some truth in that joke because what I tend not to do is over analyze when it comes to exercising gifts, talents, and things. Now, I may over-think other facets of my interactions, but not in this area of my life —*I just do it.*

However, I do suggest that if you are not accustomed to being an early riser that you get accustomed to it—make it work. Get up early in the morning before everyone in the household gets up, especially if young children are involved. Early morning is perfect time for prayer before starting your day. Ideally, there is a space, corner, or a room where you have the sanctuary and quiet that allows you to imagine and create. I have learned to silence my mobile phone and not open any apps on it before I have engaged in this sacred time with myself and God. I have also learned and exercise for my own creativity is that music is a great, great motivator. I have a playlist that I made to help me through my creative processing, and writing initiatives, albeit a book or a blog. The music/songs run the gamut and there is no one genre—including classical, operatic—some of the music is from my childhood, teenage years, music that framed special times in my life some trials and some triumphs. There are songs that remind me of my mother—songs that remind me of love, romance. Because music helps transcend my mind, soul, spirit, and even my body in some way to get moving, and to reach for emotions, memories, and inspiration to write. Music is a powerful force that stimulates the brainwaves, and proper selection of music can do wonders for stimulating creativity.

Another thing that I have learned through various experiences is that stepping out to pursue one's gifts, talents, and dreams on a broader scale is that thoughts of being or becoming financially wealthy should not be the only motivation because becoming financially wealthy is probably not going to be an immediate outcome and if that is the sole motive, it will likely deter you from moving forward in your gifts, consequently depriving others of the benefits and privilege of experiencing your gifts.

But what is assured is the wealth of fulfillment that begins to govern your ideas, decisions, and your life. The sense of being properly aligned with who and what you are meant to do is priceless, but if financial fulfillment should be an added outcome that is a wonderful added blessing.

Writing books for me has never been about some idea of grandeur of success, but rather an opportunity to share my truths, transparencies through my gift, and love for writing with the hope of inspiring, motivation, helping someone. It's grown to be about leaving something that would outlive me and shifting the paradigm for my children. Once my grandson was born, writing, and now publishing books became about leaving a legacy. I pray that I live a long robust life, but when the day comes where a grand or great grandchild does an internet search on who their grandmother was, like the caller that searched and found that I was an author, I want them to discover that, aside from corporate employment, I made other contributions to the larger landscape of life, and hopefully be proud of what they find.

> *"Each of you should use whichever gift you have received to serve others as faithful stewards, of God's grace in its various forms."*
>
> —1 Peter 4:10 (NIV)

HIGHLY VISIBLE

I recall a dream that I had once—it followed the distribution of my very first book, *"Good Relationships, Bad Relationships, What's the Common Denominator?"* It was explosive, but poorly written. It was in that book where I first revealed the truth about my uncle's attempt to sexually violate me when I was very young. I shared my memories of the night of my mother's death, and other shocking details surrounding a young girl's involvement with her "older boyfriend." It would appear that the salacious details compensated for how poorly written the book was. I exercised very little creative discretion to protect anyone, including myself. I laid it bare and doing so got some folks ire up and made me the subject of some vitriolic attacks verbal and otherwise—someone even jabbed my car tire on my new Acura TL and threw the bottle in my driveway. The only way I was sure it was behind the book is because my neighbor, who happened to know my family very well, told me who it was, and it was indeed a family member. [*"He said, the words and deeds that were spoken against you and meant to destroy you are no more."*] Following the backlash from the book, I had a dream there were people below me scuffling, fighting, and expressing hostility towards me, but I was lifted up above the fray by some invisible surface. I was sitting on this invisible surface looking down at the chaos. What this dream was communicating to me is that I would be okay. I would be protected regardless of the angry responses. What I have later come to understand is that, figuratively, I have always been lifted up which was in part how I was able to navigate through my turbulence. And never mind who dropped the ball—dropped me, because there was a growing truth within me ... "*I will take care of you.*"

Lifted up became a chapter title in a different book that I wrote, "Highly Visible", that never saw the light of day because I decided to pull the project from publishing. As the years progressed, I realized that quality of my writing was different from my "gift" to write, and I wanted to hone and refine the gift. This is an ongoing practice, and I want to believe that my future catalog of books will reflect the progress of honing my gift—this should be true for all of us as I mentioned previously.

Our gifts will make room for us (Proverbs 18:16 KJV), we should make room to grow, develop, and master those gifts and talents because in a culture when becoming a brand, being seen, heard and popular, makes it easy to find ourselves in pursuit of high visibility and validation while forgoing mastery, accountability, and intentionality of our gifts and talents. It's my hope that being highly visible before men does not take precedence over wanting to pursue excellence which reiterates the conversation between my daughter and me.

For those of you that are serious Bible readers, you are likely familiar with the story from the book of 2 Samuel that tells of a King's kid that ends up in a town equivalent to a ghetto—its definition: *land of nothing.* Mephibosheth was his name. Mephibosheth was the grandson to Saul, and when he was very young, he was crippled in his feet because someone accidently dropped him. Because of his impairment, he was put away and left in diminished conditions without any care about his existence, and he lived accordingly. I share this story because of its profound theme as well as to put an emphasis on the name of the town, Lodebar (no pasture) which always sounded like lower-the-bar to me, so I framed it as such. The narrative that I added to the story is that even when finding ourselves at a disadvantage at some point of our lives and just because someone has determined our existence isn't meaningful does not make it so. Settling for mediocrity, in my opinion, is not the most optimal outcome for anyone's life. But recently, I came across a blog via New York Magazine, titled, "Losing My Ambition" (Niazi, A., March 25, 2022). The author states, *"I have abandoned the notion of ambition to chase the middle of the road: mediocrity."* And this notion is followed up by some of the very details that I referenced earlier about people realizing that during and following the pandemic, what's important to them and life. Interestingly, the word "mediocrity" as the writer uses it can also be translated as "purpose." And that's what many are grappling with—changing perspectives that purpose may not look like the climb up the corporate ladder, but instead fulfills your soul. "*The way up and the way down are one in the same*, —Heraclitus

I also pursue writing because it fulfills my soul—it's cathartic. I may not become a bestselling author—though I would like to, but I will have done one of the many things I feel blessed to do. My hope is to connect with you as a reader just as I would if we were to meet up at a local café for coffee. And if I am to say one thing to you that compels you to move forward towards a goal, idea, or vision then I am pleased. A better version of you compels me to be a better version of myself and on and on—that's how this thing goes. At whatever the cross-section of our lives, albeit this book, an interview, or a personal encounter, the best version of me should show up, not mediocrity, and that is an ongoing evolving process of my life and purpose.

Chapter 8
A JOURNEY

We've all heard it—and I am confident many of us say it without realizing that we have regulated it to *"life is a journey"* cliché. Life is indeed a journey. For so long I did not realize the power that was packed into this simplistic expression. I viewed it merely as an expression, not realizing it is a lens through which I framed life broadly, but not personally—not specifically to how it applied to my own life. But once I embraced this concept in my personal, day-to-day, life, it changed my perspective, and consequently had a significant impact on how I framed everything else that my life entailed, and everything that I experienced—past, present, and future. And when you see your life through the lens of being a journey, more specifically *your* journey, you are less likely to be dismayed by the lack of immediate gratification, especially in a culture that promotes extreme imagery, competition, and immediate gratification.

As shared previously, I had been on the move for most of my life—starting with my early years of moving from one home to another, then one state to another—never feeling a sense of belonging or "stability." Even though I developed camaraderie, networks, and community, it was short-lived. Consequently, I did lose contact with good people, and there were some definite drawbacks financially, which are obvious adverse outcomes. This movement didn't just impact me, but my children as well. I recall someone saying to me, "This takes courage." It absolutely did, but during those years, I wasn't consciously operating out of courage; I was operating through chaos, dysfunction, and fear—though I may have looked courageous doing it—that was an unintended outcome. And this nomadic pathology surely can be attributed to my start in life, but I have grown to see some of the good that came from it—because it has absolutely developed the courage that I know I have now, and resilience I have needed to live the life that I have. It has also taught me that where you live has a critically important impact on the quality of one's life. Environment is paramount to growth, opportunities, and personal development—good or bad. So, it may not have started out as a strategy on my part—it certainly worked out that way, and I am grateful to God for it. Which further confirms my embrace of the idea of life being a journey, and how that journey is little by little, bit, by bit a part of a bigger picture.

Another outcome of my journey—learning that if one's life is not rooted in the fundamental truth that we are all a part of a larger collaboration and that there is a plan and purpose for our lives—we might miss it. This is a statement about faith. I am not sure how anyone can effectively operate, and navigate life, culture, and society with all its complexities without it. But what I do know is that I can't—and I would not ever want to because understanding where my life started, the conditions that framed my childhood pre and post my mother's death, there is no reason to believe that I would be doing what I am doing today. It is because of my faith in the consistency of God; it is because I believe that my life is part of something and someone outside of me. To contribute to the lives of my children and grandchildren is a reasonable expectation, but everything beyond that is rooted in a sense of purpose—beyond what is obvious. And again, I don't speak for my children because I know they have their own interpretations and stories to tell. However, I do know that my children are evolving, and dynamic adults—that were once on the journey with me for a time as I raised them—and though other factors, decisions and influences have contributed to their outcomes, such as relationships, friendships, college, travel, etc., I know the result of my life decisions, and movement impacted them—and not all of it is favorable. But their ability to execute grit, embrace change, familiarity with different areas different states, and strong work ethic is directly connected to having been along the journey with me for a time.

Now here's a statement that may be viewed cautiously—but I think the need or practice of seeking out stability in one's early years is overrated. I may have discovered it in a happenstance type of way—an unintended consequence per se but having done so has benefited me in ways that have enriched my life. Although I am older now nearing sixty, I do enjoy a less transient lifestyle, but I have no intentions on not continuing my journey, that will inevitably entail change. When an opportunity aligns itself with a new endeavor and vision for my life, I will respond accordingly if I am able. A journey implies movement—not stagnation, and my observation is some people confuse stagnation and complacency with stability. And this is not to say that we are not to be grateful, and content, but it is to suggest that we are multifaceted in our being, and that's what the push and pull is of being more and contributing more to life outside of a 9 to 5—and amongst other things, a global pandemic has unearthed that desire.

Instability or to be unstable seems to suggest that there may be some emotional or mental tendencies when applied to an individual, and there may be some truth in it, however that does not equate to being adverse, negative, or flawed, and I think it's that stigma that keeps many people afraid of exploring their journey. Consequently, living and leaving so much of their potential, and life experiences left on the proverbial table. Don't get me wrong, for many people this is perfectly fine, but for me, I am happy for the movement, and the journey that is my life.

TRAJECTORY

"*Where do you find the time?*" This question has since been asked of me a few times, but when asked of me in October

2021 from another caller interested in learning more about my non-profit founded in March 2021—a NPO founded to provide financial housing support for middle-aged, industrial, single women experiencing housing insecurity and/or hidden homelessness, also discovered that I published a book that same year. She asked the question, and intently awaited my response which caused an awkward silence. So, after some thought, I responded, *"I haven't found any additional time hidden anywhere, I just tend to utilize what we have"* with a slight chuckle added to break the awkwardness still lingering. It wasn't my intention to be snarky by any means, but in that moment, I felt a sense of conviction or a need to explain because I have a job, how I am finding time to write books and establish and run an NPO. But this is that mindset held by so many people—that if you work then that's all you have time to do and add in having young children (which I don't have), then that further removes the reality that you could possibly have a varied industrious and creative portfolio. And this just is not true. The founding of One Commandment Corp. Nonprofit was birthed during the global Covid:19 pandemic, a time that exposed disparities in so many areas, and simultaneously unearthed introspection, call to action, and purpose for so many. Again, I was one of those people—laid off from my new job because of the global pandemic, and one of the things I found myself asking was, *"God what should my contribution be? What aspect of my journey can serve a larger purpose in this moment?"* From that One Commandment Corp. (OCC) was birthed. The book on the other hand had been in progress for years, and just happen to be released during the pandemic shutdown. As for finding time, it's the intentional effort to utilize time wisely in a way that lends itself to making steps towards progress—even if its small steps toward multiple things.

I am multifaceted. There was a time in the not so far past when I shied away from saying that because I felt it to be boastful, but I don't feel that way any longer because it's not—it just happens to be a reality. In my preceding book, *"Becoming The Person You Told People You Were"* there is a chapter titled, *"The Real Me Authentically"* where I wrestled with defining who I am vs. what I do. And what I learned during that season of my life is that identity is paramount to embracing our authenticity. The question goes, *"Who am I?"* And answering that question honestly is liberating, and life changing. In fact, I will go as far to say, that it is necessary in order to codify *purpose* in your journey.

RENAISSANCE

Someone said to me many years ago, *"You are like a tree with many branches pointed in various directions."* I chuckled then too because I thought, *"A tree has roots— it stays put; I don't."* But I did get the point, and it was well-intended. Today what I would add to that is, though I have various branches, they are all heading in the same direction, and that is towards a desired end of a life that follows its course—adheres to the journey of fulfilling its potential. A previous director from an old job recently referred to me as a "Renaissance woman", I replied, "I'll take that." Interestingly, the conversation ended with her telling me about how she is eagerly strategizing her exit from corporate, of which she attests to having, "had enough of", and plans to join forces with a friend to start a nonprofit. She stated that she "needs to do something meaningful—a theme that seems to have evolved following the pandemic.

So, there's nothing wrong with being multifaceted, multidimensional, and a little "unstable." Though nothing should be so extreme to the point of being a detriment, but nor should anything be so detrimental as to render you stagnant. So, I repeat, life is a journey and being on a journey means movement.

I am an early riser. I have been an early riser all my life, and anything that requires extra attention, focus, or effort outside of my "job" requires making use of the early hours of the day, as early as 4:30am-5:00am... and this is where most people likely close the book. Admittingly it is not as easy for me as it once was—making this a good place to reiterate a point about *being who you say you are*. I attested to being an "earlier riser" because it's a behavior that I have carried out consistently. However, I had a recent stint where that behavior waned, and during that phase would have not been true had I written this statement before I corrected the behavior. This is the type of scenario that speaks to the title, "Be Who You Say You Are" came from. "*I am an early riser*" could not be based on a desired behavior or a past behavior, but it needed to be true of what and who I say I do and am. It's that thin line between faith and falsehood. Because what I have found in this universe of social media, is that a random act or experience is being posted to project an imagery of being or mastery of something that was merely an isolated experience—erratic at best. But the challenge I would pose is, "to be what we pretend to be." This quote from Socrates, referenced in my preceding book reads, *"The greatest way to live with honor in this world is to be what we pretend to be."* I embrace this concept. If something appeals to your sense of self enough that you would present a post as if it's indicative of your overall life and regular habits, then do it. Make time, space, and effort to really do and become in that area.

So, to do schoolwork, writing books, blogs, NPO projects, even exercise, has always required that I start early, or nothing will get done according to plan. I have gotten up as early as 2:30 or 3:00am to work on something, but that's certainly not the norm. This can be a non-starter for some people, and I understand that, but it also decreases the opportunity to *"find time"* to devote to anything other than the job, the husband and/or children that consume the rest of the day. Another thing is I am also early to bed. I get adequate rest. Sometimes sleep doesn't come as fully as I would like, especially as I get older, and biological change has its own agenda. Nevertheless, I persist at ensuring that I have adequate resting time. If a job or an employer expects that working until 8:00-10:00pm is a best practice or that answering text, calls, and emails at 11:00 at night is the "norm", that's not the job for me nor one I would remain in if that were to become the trajectory it takes. I could be in or operate in a higher title if I wanted that in exchange for autonomy over my own time, life, and creative endeavors, but I do not. And it did not take a pandemic for me to know that. I am not a corporate ladder—dream job—lifelong career type. For as long as I can remember, I have deemed a job as a means to an end, not something I cared to devote the entirety of my life to. However, it's not until recently that I have cemented a vision that the means will serve. So, I am actively working towards that vision which entails a beautifully decorated, and nostalgic Bed & Breakfast that will provide my guests with many more options than the average B&B experience, i.e., a literary space, counseling-coaching, I shared this in my last book. However, I am not willing to give too much away at this point, but this is where the vision is headed. And though I've always been of this mindset, I think this is one of the outcomes from the pandemic—the "great resignation" had more to do with the paradigm shift of people seeing their lives differently, and what it meant to be shut down—closed out and cut off. The question that arose for many of us was, "*What am I doing with my life?*" What I needed to reconcile was what I was saying vs. what I was doing. Talk vs. action. Now vs. at some point.

Now having stated all of what I have said, I am going to insert some balance here... make time to do nothing—rest, relaxation, 'chillin', bumming around, whatever term you give it, be sure to do it. There is absolutely no need to "be on" all the time, and it's certainly not the best way to manage mental and emotional health. And to do anything else such as carrying out purpose, goals, endeavors, and initiatives—subscribing time to restfulness is critically necessary. I have heard at least four people say, "I will rest when I am dead" or "Sleep is for dead people." I am stressing that is nonsense. What it can mean is that you will indeed be put to rest due to illness because of the lack thereof. I know people that are uncomfortable with restfulness because someone or something made them feel that it was a sign of laziness—again, that's nonsense. I had a relative, and for the purposes of protecting their privacy, I won't be gender or relationship specific. But they would not sleep, sat up through the night at best would nod off, but not lay down to sleep because they felt that sleep was an indication of not being useful.

Nothing comes between me and my rest. When it's time to rejuvenate, recalibrate, and to simply just do nothing, I am there!

PURPOSE

How do you know what your life's purpose is? You don't. At least not at first you don't know. One of the important things to note, and I mentioned this in my preceding book that some people are groomed, developed, and pointed in a certain direction towards their life's work—and we can compartmentalize that work into corporate or social service. I think a caveat is that when someone is groomed and ushered towards a job, or cause, it's not necessarily "their" choice, consequently not their passion or purpose. On the other side of this coin is the person that "seemingly" fumble and stumble upon their purpose—that's the group that is very likely following their personal journeys and will likely find or identify their true passion and purpose in the process.

The truth about the *"seemingly stumbling process"* is that it can look disjointed, unorganized, and even scary for onlookers, especially those that take the more stable or safe route through life and those that love you and may feel that you're doing life wrongly. There have been times where I have felt torn between two worlds being a creative visionary that allowed that to be the premise for how I wanted to pursue life. My conundrum, however, was that I was a mother who provided singly for her children. So, the initial trajectory of my life demanded that I navigate life in a traditional fashion—meaning traditional employment, and housing and provision, but my creative visionary traits pulled fiercely against the grain of that reality. So, like the generation today, I embraced that pull. For example, I ventured once to own a bookstore and it came at a cost of inconsistency some financial loss. Perhaps that should have deterred me, but it didn't, and I am grateful for that. As I have said, perhaps worded differently, that the combination of my childhood, especially following our mother's death and my genetic compilation was all foreknown by God, and as my dear friend recently reminded me of the biblical scripture, *"He knew when He knitted me in my mother's womb."* And all of me was in clear view of God. I may have had to figure me out along the way, but God has not —He's always known me.

I know that's a lot to process on the surface, but I am

confident that the coming together of Jesse LeGrande Shaw, Sr. and Dorothy Rosetta Wilson was purposed in part for bringing me forth. This is another faith statement. Now considering the tragic and tumultuous outcome of the marriage, and the fact that I am not the only child, certainly justifies anyone's counterargument. But I write through the lens of being a Believer, and that's how I view my life.

> *David had seven older brothers, yet he was the youngest that of them— anointed by Samuel while still a teenager but did not become King until age 30.* ~Samuel 16~ KJV

> *Joseph was the 2nd youngest of eleven brothers. God chose Joseph because of commitment and faithful- ness to the things of the Lord.* ~Genesis 37~ KJV

> *Long before Ester's conception God promised to bless the world through Abram's bloodline. Ester was orphaned and God saved His people through Ester. Mordecai suggested to Ester that God's hand was on her life: "Who knows, perhaps you have come to your royal position for such a time as this.* ~Ester 4:13~ CSB

Now, I know this is intense especially if biblical references aren't your thing, but I share these stories to show that despite death of parents, tragedies, and family tumult, God is never absent. And to that end, I am convinced that even before my conception God knew I'd be on that white church bus singing my heart out to Him, and no detour in my life has thwarted His plan and purpose for me.

In the recent past, while attending a family reunion in a neighborhood park, I stood in a shaded area enjoying a very passionate discussion with my cousin. He shared something with me that I only heard for the first time that day. He said, *"My dad told me (my mother's brother) that the reason your mother intended that you live with Ruth and mom (my grandmother) was because she wanted to give a part of herself back to them—she wanted them to do for you, to take care of you like they wanted to do for her."* I will use creative discretion and not speak to any of the details and speculation, that I don't know as truth, that swirled around about what seemed to be an estranged relationship between my mother and *some* of her family—mainly her mother. But him sharing that with me, though not validated, re-shaped a lot of thoughts and ideas that I held. It was after that very day when I committed to carrying out a life that would honor that beautiful and courageous woman that I don't doubt one bit was managing her own broken heartedness and trauma—even before her marriage.

Chapter 9
ONE COMMANDMENT CORP
"Love Thy Neighbor as Thyself"

In my last book I concluded with a summary of how I see myself moving forward with my gifts, talents, and entrepreneurial ideas—founding a non-profit organization (NPO), was not on that list. Interestingly, that is the thing about becoming, and being who you say you are, it's an ever-evolving process, when you continue to open yourself up to growth, ideas, and God's will—and have the gumption to actually do what is forming for you to do—even though it (the vision) may not be completely laid out in front of you—but you know something more or other than is awaiting you. One of the core messages from "Becoming The Person You Told People You Were" was oftentimes you will hear other people tell you what they see in, or who they thought you were when you walked in a room, or you are consistently being asked to do a particular thing—provide a particular service, like prepare food, pick out outfits for other people, decorate other people homes. Or statements like, *"You would make a good teacher, counselor"*, *"interior designer"*, etc. These things are nudges—they are whispers revealing your gifts and purpose to you. And oftentimes we can miss it if we don't have an ear to hear or an eye to see what's present and available for us to evolve accordingly.

One thing I did learn from that social media "writing community" that I joined is how much writers innately have in common—they love journals, books, bookstores, fancy ink pens and oftentimes they are avid readers, and generally those fetishes seemingly existed before they made a connection to wanting to be a writer. There is something to that, but you have to view it through a spiritual lens.

There is a scripture where God ask Moses, *"What is that in your hand?"* Exodus 42 KJV. It was an ordinary staff that Moses used every day until He did what God gave him to do, and that staff went from being ordinary to extraordinary changing the course of Moses' mission and the lives of everyone in his orbit. That's what it is to utilize our gifts and talents towards the desired end that God has for us. But complacency, fear, and laziness are counter forces that will obstruct that forward movement. And quite honestly, if that is the case, only God can change your mind about it.

So, like everyone else, experiencing the pandemic and having time to reset, reevaluate, revisit, and literally revise their lives—the same applied to me. The time spent reprioritizing what was important and what wasn't flooded my quiet time in isolation during the pandemic even though I was active creating content, like podcasts with colleagues, blogging, making live steam videos on topics ranging from caring for your physical and mental health, eating well, in-house exercise plans, etc. But what I sought to know most was what had my life's journey given me to share—what would have been my contribution to the larger scale of life—if things were to never return to normal?

I am not sure that there's anyone on the planet that hasn't heard of Tyler Perry, but in the event there's one. Tyler Perry is now a mega, movie and playwright, producer, actor, philanthropist, billionaire from New Orleans, born in September of 1969 that was once a homeless man living out of his car near the Georgia State Route highway 166 sign and exit that now bears his name. Now, I don't dare include this remarkable rags to riches story to make any comparison to my outcomes vs his, but I share it because it too serves as an example of how on the other side of time there is a future version of every one of us and we owe it to ourselves and certainly to our Creator to see that process through because time and chance happens for us all.

> *"I have seen something else under the sun:*
> *The race is not to the swift or the battle to*
> *the strong, nor does food come to the wise or*
> *wealth to the brilliant or favor to the learned,*
> *but time and chance happen to them all."*
>
> —Ecclesiastes 9:11 NIV

One Commandment Corp, is the response to my question during prayer: *"God what has my life's journey taught, given me, placed in my hand that I can offer back in service?"*

It's important to note here, the scenario returning from Portland, Maine, and Canada was not my first experience with temporary homelessness. When the job in Georgia ended, I spent a stint of time sleeping in my car as well. Staying securely housed was one of my biggest life challenges for various reasons. As a teenage single mom, I worked. I never accepted government resources therefore never having any type of subsidized anything—food, housing, daycare, none of it. I chose that because I never wanted to be subjected to the whims of government. Additionally, I never wanted to be pigeonholed in a system designed to keep you there. I know an abundance of people that did receive government assistance and navigated their way out to amazing quality lifestyles, but I also know an abundance of people that did not—and I did not want to risk being in the latter group. So, I lived in communities with the best school districts, so that my children could attend them—that was my mission, to get them through public schools in good districts, and I accomplished that. Yes, it came at the cost of rents, daycare, and other things that I struggled to afford. I knew if I could hang in there, though my children might come through it with some stories of hard times, they would have benefited from the offerings of optimal curriculum, and other opportunities that well-funded public schools offer which would ultimately equip them for formal education in the end—and that was accomplished. So, like I said, I can't tell their stories for them because they aren't for me to tell but being along the journey with me for a while had its pros and cons. My only hope is that they feel the pros outweighed the cons.

So, housing insecurity for me as a working, industrious, and formally educated woman was once a thing for me. That's the thread that runs through OCC—it's my offering—and reasonable service.

A NPO founded—birthed out of what has once been my reality. I would later learn and see, it's the realities of so many women alike. Just within eight months of OCCs establishment we housed our first candidate. I met her sitting out in the hallway of my employer trying to use her laptop to apply for a job. However, I felt a need to ask her if she was okay, although it's customary for me to speak to everyone I see—there was a sensing in my spirit about her. I invited her back to my office and asked if I could help her with getting her application done, suspecting this would unfold the story I knew was there.

She is a Ghana native and has lived in the United States for more than twenty years. According to her, she was once a married woman, to an Engineer who lives in New Jersey with whom she had two young twin boys. Her husband brutally beat her often, but the last time he threw her out on the steps in the freezing cold left for dead. For whatever reason he was able to win custody of the boys, and consequently receive child support from her. She lost her (low-paying job) as many of us did due to Covid:19, but in her case the person that she provided care for died of the virus, and consequently she was out of work, and soon out of money. She would eventually resort to living inside of her furniture storage unit, where she was staying when I met her. For days I asked her to keep coming back to my office, so that I could take her to lunch and work with one of our hiring managers to get her work which would eventually be successful. What happened next could only be God's sovereignty.

Before moving into my current home, I did a house share renting the lower apartment area of a three-story townhome. The family and owner lived in the upper portion of the home. So, by way off OCC's Board members, she was interviewed to determine if she'd be eligible for financial housing support, and the Board unanimously approved housing support of a security deposit, rent for the first two weeks of her tenure allowing her time to get her first paycheck. She was able to rent the in-house apartment that I once occupied.

Although an amazing testament of OCC's purpose and mission, she did not like or succeed being in the job and was asked to resign within her first 90 days, consequently having to surrender the housing we acquired for her. And though we could not recover the funds we provided for her scrubs, personal items, and the required footwear for her job, we had in place a contract with the landlord to return the donor dollars used for the security deposit.

As I wrote this paragraph, I could see the hand of God clearly. She lost the job, returned to sleeping in the storage unit—within a short time after that her mother died in

Ghana. Her pain was so deep she could not form words—I could relate to that. So, I asked that she stay in touch to let me know how she's doing. She returned to Ghana to handle her mother's affairs, and when she returned, she called to tell me that she was okay, back from Ghana, and in desperate need of employment again. Just a couple of months prior to this—my employer implemented a new business model which resulted in me being switched from my original entity—where she too had been originally hired. To be fully transparent, I was livid about the change. So much so, I cried literal tears because of it. The transition seemed to be poorly timed, it was poorly executed and disruptive to the course of my work. But what I never imagined is I would be able to get her rehired as a result. Had I remained assigned to my previous entity, this would not have been an option. So, she's now gainfully re-employed, enjoying her job, and the hiring manager loves her. You can't make this stuff up—this is real—this is God.

MATTERS OF THE HEART

Another outcome that resulted out of the uncertainty, fear, and isolation, of the Covid:19 pandemics, put in clearer view for me that life is fragile, what's important and what's not, and literally being able to take a breath has new value to me. I love and enjoy an occasional two-step every now and again, but I have vowed that from this day to my last I will dance every opportunity I get. I will laugh hard and often, and I will love those that let me with all the love I can muster up. This too is why completing this book was necessary because the idea of "having plenty of time" has shifted and taking for granted that *tomorrow is promised* feels irresponsible to me now. Like many of us, I too lost loved-ones, friends, and family to Covid:19 and its mutations that continue to linger.

So, it's been a plan for a while now, to do something big to celebrate my sixtieth birthday. I think it will either be a large formal gathering or a trip out of the country. But because I experienced during the pandemic a few people that arose to the top for me, I didn't want to wait. I got unexpected phone calls from specific family members checking in to ask how I was holding up during quarantine. A few new friends and others that have been friends for years, even if it were via phone, zoom or social media. A couple showed up in person, though masked and distanced—they visited. So, as you might imagine this only crystalized the importance of their love and friendship. Because of that, I decided not to wait another year to do a big birthday celebration. But instead of a formal elaborate gathering—it was an intimate dinner party where I prepared all the food including desserts, because preparing a big dinner for family is my love language. I purchased very inexpensive gifts for all my guests as a token of my appreciation for each one of them. They not only enriched my life when it was needed most, but they did not think it was too much to ask that they drive three hours, and for some of them, stay over at a hotel, so we could have a nice Christmas Eve-morning breakfast that I would prepare. My guests were family and friends that I love deeply, and grew closer to during the pandemic and I wanted them to know it. My guests were strategically selected, not only because I had limited space to host them but because they all hold a special place in my heart. I refused to wait three years to gather with them. I could not think of any better way to spend my fifty-seventh birthday than with them.

Now, here we are already—another birthday has come and gone. December 23rd. —I turned 58 which sounds surreal to me. I feel that I got here at the speed of light even with all of the life happenings in-between.

I can honestly say that I had not felt a whole lot different from forty-seven to fifty-seven—naturally I look older than I did at forty-seven, but I maintained a very robust walking and bike riding routine even through the pandemic. Some days I rode as much as ten to twelve miles and alternatively walked much of the same. I thought this worth mentioning, because being who we say we are, becoming who we want to be—entails having a pulse on our physical health as well—and until recently I took this for granted.

That said, I somehow translated exercise, gym member- ship, and selective healthy food choices to being adequate, and as long as I felt good; I was good. And just in case any of you think the same because I know people that do—it's not necessarily true. And though I have facetiously asserted that hypertension (high blood pressure), and high cholesterol are code for being a Black person, there may be a tiny bit truth in that—and I have not been exempted from that reality.

Shocked when my numbers came up as they did this year and hearing a doctor say, "*Your cholesterol numbers are very concerning, and I am not comfortable letting you leave without a prescription."* That was a watershed moment for me because in that moment the seriousness on her face confirmed that I can't cycle, walk, or weight-lift this away which I thought I was doing. Nervously, I asked what this meant? It's a matter of the heart: *"It means you could be at risk of a heart attack"*, she said. I immediately thought back to a time when we were losing my oldest sister due to a failed surgical procedure, and the physician at that time mentioned something about my sister's heart—inferring it had something to do with why her surgery failed. I don't remember the exact comment, but I do remember it being suggested that her sisters and daughters should probably get checked. I heard it and for some reason dismissed it—perhaps finding comfort in denial. But what I know for sure now—and no longer afraid to confront—is to be healthy is not just outwardly, but inwardly as well, and that's a reality that fifty-eight has brought along with it for me.

So, this feels to be my last book for a while unless God puts something in my spirit. Although, there's a slight possibility that I'll move forward with publishing the "love story" I wrote which was a very different type of writing style for me, but if I must say so myself, it's a great work of storytelling—a beautiful reenactment of a love story. So, I will wait to see if I feel compelled to bring that forth.

And yes, it's true when I say, if God does not do another thing for me, He has done enough. I really know what that statement means in my life today. But there's something I want to ensure that you take away from this book—what helped me exercise the courage to leave an abusive marriage is because Tina Turner shared her journey in a book. How I mustered up and developed the self-esteem and self-respect that would allow me to still rise despite all of the faltering and messy days of my life when I felt like it might easier to die, is because Dr. Maya Angelou shared her journey in a book. My awakening towards exercising the fortitude of becoming and being a woman for God is because Joyce Meyer shared her journey in a book. It's because of this, I find myself willing to share my journey along the way with the hope that within the sphere of influence that God affords me—something I share through writing will change an adverse perspective, behavior or outcome in someone's life—at best be a seed that someone else will come along and water to bring about a flourishing into the best version of themselves and that's the benefit of writing for me—using my gift to do what was done for me is how all of our lives intersect—so we all remain diligent and intentional about helping someone else after we've been helped.

So, while I know it's a process that will continuously evolve as we navigate human struggles and contradictions, but nevertheless, I implore you to go ahead and do what you say you do—be who you say you are, because you can—and yes it is a journey—and no journey is without challenges, complexities and human error, but you and your gifts are an answer to someone else's promise. So, please keep moving—and then help someone else do the same.

Chapter 10
A HALF DOZEN OR SO OR NINE MONTHS TO GROW

Michelle Obama; Gabrielle Union; Mariah Carey; Brook Shields; Tyra Banks; Angela Bassett and Chrissy Tiegen are just a few of the famous names that we can put a face with of women that have been transparent about their struggles with infertility—or an inability to carry a pregnancy to term, if they could conceive at all. I want to share another side—perhaps another perspective of this reality.

Not every face and name are known—not every woman is famous, wealthy, or willing to share this sensitive reality. And for some women it may even be a root of bitterness or resentment—for others it can stir up an obsessive-like behavior and pathology over other women's pregnancies or children. I share this because I was the object of both extremes. I had one woman who could no longer conceive randomly sharing pictures of my youngest, (infant) daughter with strangers and referencing her ambiguously as if to omit that she wasn't hers—it was brought to my attention for awareness. I had another scenario where a woman that could not conceive or carry simulate hitting my infant in the face with a crab mallet when I approached her with my one-month-old beautiful baby girl, nestled in the nook of my curled arm—swaddled in a beautiful pink-white crochet blanket to show her my latest point of pride and joy. She, blurted out, "*You didn't have anything better to do than to have another baby!*" Then proceeded to simulate hitting her in the head with the mallet. I will use creative discretion concerning how the rest of that scenario played out. But what I remembered was roughly a year and a half prior—this same woman tearfully said to me as I made a reference to my, now, middle daughter, "*You are a good mother. I can't have a baby even if someone were to put it inside of me.*" So, I knew that the alcohol induced response to my newborn was a response of resentment, jealousy, bitterness—and depression. The mental health component of this reality should not be trivialized.

Nor is this topic intended to shame any women experiencing these emotions—in fact it's just the opposite—it's to say, that you are not alone—we see and support you. But, consequently; I think these emotions are masked more than any other facet of this conundrum—they are not discussed as openly as they could be—therefore exasperating the secret embarrassment some women feel. For other women—they are ashamed for various reasons, that they are unable to carry a pregnancy i.e., they question their womanhood—although one has nothing to do with the other, but that doesn't negate the validity of those feelings—so stigmas persist. But in other instances where many women had the good fortune and resources to afford In vitro fertilization (IVF) or the blessing of surrogacy—their dreams, desire, and willingness to have children, and a family were realized because on the other side of this conundrum was a young woman capable and willing to donate her eggs or to be a surrogate.

The reason I have decided to include this chapter is-because I hope to invoke thought, compassion, conversation and maybe even "involvement."

Even as we fight for a "Woman's Right to Choose", (which I support). I also empathize with any woman that would give anything to be able to conceive and can't—to carry and can't. I know women in my life, and networks that can't. And it wasn't until I met the first of those women that I realized what I took for granted, as being as natural as breathing—was someone else's physical impossibility.

I think pregnancy is beautiful—the entire process. Remembering various times of being told, "You look beautiful pregnant." Well, I know that wasn't always true, but I felt beautiful, and that's what was permeating—how I *felt*. If I were happily married, and wealthy; I would have had several children, but as a single, and later a divorced woman—my purse strings tied up at three—though I birthed four—with one dying prematurely. Nevertheless, absolutely could not expand any further beyond the three. But I wanted more under the right conditions, nevertheless time and chance played its hand. So, this one thing will remain on the list of things I always wanted to do—the thing I let slip through my fingers because I either got distracted, sidetracked, or just procrastinated, therefore not elevating it to the level of importance I wished I had—consequently missing the window of opportunity, to have enrolled in an egg donor or surrogacy program. I utterly wanted to make this a part of my legacy, and a blessing realized for someone else.

As a young woman, I am convinced that I was blessed by the fertility "gods", and I realized that I was blessed once meeting one woman after another that could not conceive children, while I took for granted the ease by which I could. So much-so, that I could count on my children being born precisely on their due dates because I knew their conception dates—allowing for a 24–48-hour variance.

I read in Will Smith's memoir, that his wife, Jada Pinkett Smith knew within the seconds that she was pregnant, (Smith, W., 2021). Some thought and still 'meme' it as ridiculousness—but I totally know of that reality. Oddly, the last time this crossed my mind was in my early fifties, by which time, was moot because of my age.

However, on December 22, 2022, the day before my fifty-eighth birthday; I underwent a total hysterectomy due to uterine fibroids.

Now, having shared this; I don't want to glaze over the adverse history of the pattern of excessive hysterectomy procedures performed on Black women and other women of color. If it's something you want to know more about;

I encourage you to do some research—if for no other reason than to be informed. When I was a young girl, I remember several women in my orbit talking about having under-gone or having a procedure scheduled. During this era, it would appear that the procedures had a more nefarious intent. Even today, I am not sure we have totally mediated the targeted race (s), and capitalistic gain agendas concerning this phenomenon. In fact, in the very recent past I happened to be on a leadership call with a medical institution when the unit where these surgeries are performed was referenced as, "Our money-making procedures." Definitely a tone death statement and one where *"saying the quiet part out loud"*, was surely a faux pas. So, before I digress from sharing historical information; I want to share a couple of poignant facts for awareness:

> ~According to Women's History website, "In 1961, Fannie Lou Hamer received a hysterectomy by a white doctor without her consent while undergoing surgery to remove a uterine tumor", (womenshistory.org, 2022).

> ~According to a Washington Post online article, "J. Marion Sims—a doctor that performed unauthorized and non-consented hysterectomy on enslaved women without anesthesia because according to him; Black women don't feel pain", (washingtonpost.com, 2022).

As for me, I voluntarily opted to have a total hysterectomy for which I was afraid of the anesthesia—not the procedure. Following an annual gynecological visit—an exam would reveal that I was carrying one fibroid the size of a grapefruit and several other smaller ones surrounding it. But it would not be until after the surgery that, (I elected to have), when the final number of fourteen in total would be confirmed. As stoic and composed as the surgeon had been during my visits, for the first time, when he stood at my bedside in recovery, I saw his facial expression (forehead) contort, when he stated, "*You had fourteen fibroids.*" In my groggy state, I responded, "*That's massive*" and the surgeon responded, "*In medical terms, yes that's massive.*" He proceeded to show me pictures for me to see for myself—which gave me the chills—but it was when he pointed to my ovaries in the picture, and said, "Your ovaries were in pristine condition—they were both optimal", was when I quickly turned my head to hide my teary eyes that were filling up. But in keeping with the procedure, he removed one of my ovaries. I was saddened, reminded, and now deeply regretting, that I let the window of opportunity to assist another woman in her ability to have children close—another woman who wasn't as fortunate as I had been to be blessed with fertility, or the ability to carry a pregnancy. And now that the ability to do so, without question, no longer exist for me—it's my hope to be a part of the larger conversation. A conversation that contributes to debunking the stigmas and shame around infertility, and perhaps stimulate thought and stir up additional conversations, sensitivity, and compassion within my sphere of reach for those women that may be a possibility to another woman's impossibility.

There was an inside joke recently following my

procedure of *"Dang! You mean all this time I could have tapped you on the shoulder to borrow some eggs."* Hilarious to the point of laughing tears—but yet a truth.

I decided to add this chapter because it would appear that my hope of starting conversations within my sphere of reach and perhaps enlightening someone towards this end has been realized. Prior to deciding to include this topic in this book, I wrote it as a blog and received several responses—more than I have from any blog I have ever posted. One reader shared, she and her friends have started talking about it after reading the blog, and two of them have decided to look into the process of becoming egg donors, and they have since taken steps towards doing just that.

So, while this topic and chapter may feel a tad awkwardly placed, perhaps even a bit intrusive—it is okay, because it too provides insight into matters of the heart, soul and spirit that are equally as important to one's life's trajectory and legacy. Also, this further confirms for me as a writer about those matters of heart, soul, and spirit—that reaching somebody outside of my immediate circle and network is indeed the reason why I write—even if that somebody is just one body—then I am fulfilled.

May God bless and keep you Dear Reader until we meet again.

#ABetterYouIsABetterMe

> "For I know the plans I have for you, declares the Lord, plans to prosper you and not to harm you, plans to give you hope and a future."
>
> Jeremiah 29:11 (KJV)

Your Thoughts…

_____
_____
_____
_____
_____
_____
_____
_____
_____
_____
_____
_____
_____
_____
_____
_____
_____

Dorothy Rosetta Shaw

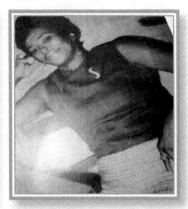

Jesse LeGrande Shaw, Sr.

Michael Leroy Shaw #9

Michael & me

*Last time I saw him
Thanksgiving, 2016*

Resources

Non-profit Website:
Onecommandmentcorp.com
Onecommandmentnonprofit@gmail.com

Author's Website:
SelfLove🌷 (bestselfcys.com)

Blogsite:
#ABetterYouIsABetterMe (abyiabm.blogspot.com)

About the Author

Christie Y. Shaw works as a Human Resources Professional. A mother of three; grandmother of one. Christie's passion is to encourage personal development, and healthy self-esteem. Currently a resident in Alexandria, VA Christie heads up her own job coaching service where the goal through mentoring, training, and support, to assist possible candidates in gaining sustainable employment. Christie's currently a PhD Candidate in I/O Psychology. Also, the Founder of a non-profit established to provide financial housing support for single, industrious, women experiencing housing insecurity.

References

Butler, T. (2007. Getting Unstuck. Harvard Business School Publishers. Boston Massachusetts

Huffington Post, (Mazza, E., September 6, 2022),

Niazi, A., March 25, 2022, *Losing My Ambition*

Perry, F. C. (1993). *History of Baldt Anchor and Chain 1901-1975*. Retrieved from http://oldchesterpa.com/baldt_anchor_history.htm

Shaw, C. Y. (2018). *Becoming The Person, You Told People You Were*. Christian Faith Publishing, Inc. Meadville, PA.

Smith, W. C. (2021). WILL. Pinguin Press. New York, New York.

Thomas Nelson, Inc. (1984, 1977). Holy Bible, King James, Online BibleGateway, CSB, ESV & NIV Versions.

Link:

SCIWAY. (2018). Shaw Plantation Williamsburg County South Carolina. Retrieved from https://south-carolina-plantations.com/williamsburg/shaw.html

The Guardian, (Shoard, C., Sept., 5, 2022)

CPSIA information can be obtained
at www.ICGtesting.com
Printed in the USA
JSHW081734170523
41779JS00002B/99